THE
BREAD
OF GOD

Nurturing a Eucharistic Imagination

TONY KELLY, C.Ss.R.
FOREWORD BY M. BASIL PENNINGTON

Liguori
LIGUORI, MISSOURI

Published by Liguori Publications
Liguori, Missouri
www.liguori.org
www.catholicbooksonline.com

Library of Congress Cataloging-in-Publication Data

Kelly, Tony.
    The bread of God / Nurturing a eucharistic imagination / Tony Kelly.
        p. cm.
    Includes bibliographical references.
    ISBN 0-7648-0711-0 (pbk.)
    1. Lord's Supper—Catholic Church. 2. Imagination—Religious aspects—Catholic Church. 3. Spiritual life—Catholic Church. 4. Catholic Church—Doctrines. I. Title.

BX2215.3 .K45 2001
234'.163—dc21   00–049785

Printed in the United States of America
05 04 03 02 01   5 4 3 2 1
First Edition

CONTENTS

FOREWORD

The Eucharist has had many meanings for the People of God. Not so long ago, it was an awful Majesty worshiped from afar, approached only rarely. The saintly father, Pius X, invited his children to the table. With the ongoing action of the Spirit with the Church, we came closer and closer until another saintly pontiff, John XXIII, help break away the encrustations of centuries. Again, as in the early Church, the Eucharist means the People of God gathered around the table, eagerly entering into Communion not only sacramentally but with one another in reality. This remarkable book urges us along this same path, helping us to not only understand but to experience what the Eucharist calls us to.

The Sacred Scriptures are full of stories and images of all kinds. When the message is too great to be contained within the restraints of definable concepts, authors resort to poetics. So too did the Divine Author. In an outreaching love, he came to be with us to tell us personally of the kingdom from whence he came. In this revealing, he resorted to parables and images. Ultimately he himself in his humanity is the sacrament, the outward expression of the inner reality. And he left himself sacramentally in our midst in the Eucharist. It is the message of this Sign, who is a Person of Infinite Love, that our author seeks to help us not only hear but also experience and to live more fully in the domain of the imagined.

We know as Christians that we have been baptized *into* Christ, made one with him. We are called to be Christ in the world today. But as we seek to live the Christ-life to the full, many of us never think of entering into the imagination of Christ. We have heard, "Let this mind be in you which was in Christ Jesus"—and have sought to think as Christ thinks and place his value on things. But if we reflect, we realize that we humans are more influenced in our daily living by the images that are fed to our eyes and ears, that dwell in our memory and call forth emotions than we are influenced by our rational thoughts. It does not take much reflection on the gospels to realize how fully cognizant Jesus was of this as he sought to teach us by stories and signs that appeal to our imaginations.

For many a reader, Father Kelly is going to open a whole domain for entering fruitfully and effectively into the Christ-life. For this reason, this is a most valuable volume. It can be life-transforming. If the Eucharist, holy Communion, who is a Person as well as a Symbol, is allowed, under the tutelage of this gifted insightful author, to become the Master-Symbol of our lives, we will find a transcending unity that will satisfy our deepest longings while inspiring and empowering us to live in the reality of our oneness with all our sisters and brothers in Christ.

The author makes us realize that this creative unity of "the fruit of the earth and the work of human hands" with the divine self-giving challenges us to a deeper awareness of our responsibility for the ecological well-being of our planet, the earth we constantly mold by the work of our hands. It depends on us as good stewards to assure it is allowed to remain a powerful and beautiful sign of the divine munificence.

If we allow it, I am sure that the reading of this significant volume will not only ground our lives more richly and heighten our ecological awareness. It will profoundly affect our prayer as it leads us into the domain of compassion. For in Eucharist we not only turn with Christ to the Begetter of the Universe, but we are challenged to give ourselves with Christ to all our sisters and brothers through space and time—to give ourselves as life-cherishers. Our world is not the anonymous and indifferent place that science seems to reveal but, in truth, it is the homeland and heartland of an infinitely loving God. For the Father and Son with their Holy Spirit have come to make their home within us. The incarnate Word makes our sufferings his own through this sacrifice truly presenced in the Eucharist even while he gives us the assurance of final transformation by his Resurrection. The Eucharist not only brings all this to mind. It nourishes this reality within us. The Eucharist educates—in the fullest meaning of that word—our imaginations, minds, and hearts to embrace all in all its fullness in its oneness in Christ Jesus.

BASIL PENNINGTON, OCSO
HOLY SPIRIT ABBEY, CONYERS, GEORGIA

PREFACE

I have used the words *Eucharistic Imagination* in the subtitle of this book. I realize that such wording might suggest a tendency to back off from the objective reality of Christ's presence to us in the sacrament of the Eucharist, and to retreat into some kind of private fantasy world. Nothing could be further from my intent. The point I am trying to make is this: because the Eucharist is uniquely the sacrament of Christ's self-gift to the Church, because it is centered on the "real presence" of the Lord in the midst of the Church, it nourishes not only our bodies and souls with the food and drink of eternal life but also in so doing it enters into the way we imagine the truths of faith—Christ Jesus himself, the God he reveals, the Church he calls into being, our mission as Christians in the world and, indeed, the universe itself as God's creation.

It might have been wiser to speak of eucharistic "theology." But since theology is a critical intellectual exercise in the service of faith, its primary purpose is to promote understanding—not, therefore, to inspire imagination. To some degree, theology attempts to move beyond images in its effort to express a critical and coherent understanding of what faith professes. Even a good theology may fail to grip the imagination, if only for the reason that this is not its purpose. Needless to say, I am not adopting an anti-theological stance. I hope, then, that it will be obvious to any reader that I am using the best resources of the theology of the past and present. Nonetheless, I am aiming at something more concrete, vital, and more immediately pastoral. Low-level theology? Perhaps; but, I suggest, only in the sense that Christian experience, feeling, response, and commitment are the fertile ground from which creative theology arises. The images, symbols, sacraments of faith embody the meanings that theology endlessly explores. Hence, "eucharistic imagination."

Another option would be to speak in terms of eucharistic *devotion*. In its oldest sense, that word might be closer to what concerns me. On the other hand, it is a word that has not traveled well in our contemporary vocabulary. It too easily suggests an individual attitude that is not sufficiently beholden to the public liturgy of the Church. It is more likely to connote "Visits to the Blessed Sacrament" than a liturgical involvement in the community's celebration of the Eucharist. It so happens that I have not the slightest problem with "making visits to the Blessed Sacrament"—how could I, as a Redemptorist and a son of Saint Alfonso di Liguori, founder of our congregation, dismiss such a tradition of devotion? His *Visits to the Blessed Sacrament* are among the great classics of eucharistic piety. Indeed, I am confident that quiet prayer before the tabernacle or with the Blessed Sacrament exposed remains a valuable extension of what I am here calling the eucharistic imagination. Such practices cultivate a sense of the enduring quality of Christ's gift and presence and lead to a deeper assimilation of the meaning of the Eucharist. But such devotional practices are an extension of the "eucharistic imagination" I intend to explore, not a substitute for it.

Well, why not write *spirituality*? That is a more popular word in our current religious language, and, to some degree, a slippery one. It has migrated from a faith-related usage, for example, the various "spiritualities" of religious orders, to mean something more general and amorphous. Two reasons incline me to prefer *imagination* in its place. First, it is a word generally favored in situations where explicit Christian faith is not regarded as an option: spirituality, yes! Church, no! " New Age" spirituality, say, suggests a level of creativity on the level of cosmic consciousness or some new mode of self-awareness. In contrast, the Church—written off as a dull example of "organized religion"—is presumed not to be interested in such matters. I would contend that it is—or should be; and that the Eucharist, "the summit and source of the life of the Church," is a unique inspiration in this regard—even to the extent of a "cosmic consciousness" and an "ecological awareness" in the light of Christ as will appear later. By using the word, *imagination*, rather than *spirituality*, I feel a closer link to the living imagination of the Church as it enacted in the liturgy; and to the imagination of Jesus himself who expressed his self-gift to us in a eucharistic form.

The other reservation I have regarding the use of *spirituality* in its current sense is that it tends to be self-regarding, as though it were "my spirituality"—a cultivation of my "self-awareness." It is as though the "self" were an enclosed, inviolable, all-sufficient entity—a self-sufficiency that can be extended but not disturbed. In contrast, the imagination that the Eucharist provokes is radically disturbing for any such version of self-sufficiency. Christians live from a gift—a disturbing thought in itself. The form and nourishment of such a gift is the self-giving love of Christ. He gave us himself, and with that invites us to share in his imagination. It opens into new relationships—with those with whom we celebrate the Eucharist, with all members of the Church, and the whole world of God's love (John 3:16), and with the whole of creation. In such an imagination, we are always living beyond ourselves, for our true and final life is Christ himself.

Finally, *imagination* as I will be using it implies something dramatic and restless. The Eucharist stimulates faith to imagine the world "otherwise." It is not a concession to agnosticism for even the most committed believer to pose the question, What if the mysteries we celebrate in the Eucharist are true? What if Christ were truly and really present in this way? What if eternal life had already begun in the eating and drinking of the body and blood of Christ? Could it be really so that our world is so penetrated and possessed by God that the gift of all gifts comes to us through the transformation of fruit of our earth and work of our human hands? Is the Eucharist, in the shrouded and ambiguous form of our present existence, really the form of eternal life, and of communion with all in the Trinitarian life of God? For the believer to ask such questions need not indicate any lapse into agnosticism. It is just that no one of us can appreciate the eucharistic reality in its every dimension all at once, and that every experience of the "real presence" of Christ leads the Christian conscience to acknowledge areas of its "real absence"—not because of any reservation on the part of Christ but because our reception of what he offers is always limited and subject to the demands of a greater conversion to "the way, and the truth, and the life" (John 14:6). To follow that way more directly, to hold to that truth more clearly, to live that life more generously, express the best of Christian intentions, even though we all fall short. Still, we are brought to the sharp point of the most basic questions, If the Eucharist makes truly present to us "the life of the world," why not live now? Why not live the truth that is so present? Why not let our imaginations catch up with the reality and expand to its proportions?

In this effort to expand our experience of the Eucharist, I begin by linking the eucharistic imagination to the imagination of Christ and of the Church, contrasting it to other forms of imagining and the kinds of "virtual reality" they tend to promote.

Chapters two to five are explicitly biblical. They examine how the eucharistic imagination is promoted by Paul in his dealings with the Corinthians, by Luke in his account of the disciples' journey to Emmaus, and by John in chapters six and thirteen of his Gospel. While a little book like this must be selective, I do make the point that, while biblical scholars search into the various eucharistic references in the Scriptures, the Eucharist itself, in the ongoing life of the People of God, is site and the source of our deepest contact with what the New Testament witnesses to.

Chapter six connects the movement of Christian conversion to various themes and attitudes that characterize the eucharistic imagination: sacrifice, communion, judgment, praise, and love. This leads into considerations of the Eucharist as the sacrament of hope, and, perhaps surprisingly, as a form of Christian ecological consciousness and responsibility—in chapters seven and eight respectively. Chapter ten considers the Eucharist as a manifestation of the presence of the Holy Spirit, a theme that should ideally be extended much further. Then I add a reflection on the Lord's Day as the eucharistic hallowing of time. By way of conclusion, I offer, in free verse form, what I call "Eucharistic Imagining." Perhaps some readers might be inspired to do something like this for themselves, the better to bring out the imaginative depth that the sacrament of the Eucharist contains, even as it permits and inspires an endless number of expressions.

The unifying thread of these various themes is the imaginative vision and creativity the Eucharist inspires. It affects the way we read our image-shaped world. It allows for a properly imaginative dimension in our understanding of the Scriptures. It animates the movement of Christian conversion, highlighting the values and priorities in that continuing journey. It sustains hope and a sense of wonder at our planetary existence. It helps us discern the presence and action of the Holy Spirit. It makes us appreciate time in a new way. Finally, it leaves each one of us to do our own imagining in the different graces of our individual lives.

While I think there is a defensible logic in the order of this presentation, readers can let their own imaginations guide them to whatever interests them in whatever order.

I am acutely aware of the many splendid theological works that have influenced me in the writing of this book, and which would prove useful for those who wish to take their studies further.

As an example of the heartwarming piety of the past, *The Holy Eucharist* by Saint Alphonsus himself (or Alfonso, if we prefer the Italian), Eugene Grimm, trans. (Brooklyn: Redemptorist Fathers, 1934) is a collection of the most popular works (*The Sacrifice of Jesus Christ, Visits to the Blessed Sacrament, Meditations for the Octave of Corpus Christi, Novena to the Sacred Heart, The Practice of the Love of Jesus Christ*). The liturgical and cultural concerns of today demand, of course, a different emphasis; but it is certainly a challenge for the eucharistic imagination of our time to retrieve the intense, ecstatic personalism and practical accents of that past period of Christian piety. In the authoritative *Catechism of the Catholic Church* (Sydney and New York: St. Pauls, 1995), a particularly valuable section is found in Part 2, "The Celebration of the Christian Mystery," 277–310; 334–354 (of the pocketbook edition).

For a scholarly yet accessible biblical emphasis, I commend Eugene La Verdiere, *The Eucharist in the New Testament and the Early Church* (Collegeville, Minn.: The Liturgical Press, 1996), and Francis J. Moloney, *A Body Broken for a Broken People*: *Eucharist in the New Testament* (Peabody, Mass.: Hendrickson, 1997). On a pastoral level, Cardinal Roger Mahoney, *Gather Faithfully Together: Guide for Sunday Mass* (Chicago: Liturgy Training Publications, 1997) is most successful.

For perspectives in sacramental theology, a standard reference is David N. Power, *Sacrament: The Language of God's Giving* (New York: Crossroad, 1999). A remarkable work for its social and cultural concern is William T. Cavanaugh, *Torture and the*

Eucharist: Theology, Politics, and the Body of Christ (Oxford: Blackwell, 1998). For a strong moral and ethical emphasis, see E. Byron Anderson and Bruce T. Morrill, eds., *Liturgy and the Moral Self: Humanity at Full Stretch Before God* (Collegeville, Minn.: The Liturgical Press, 1998). Then, there is the most stimulating book by James Alison, *Raising Abel: The Recovery of the Eschatological Imagination* (New York: Crossroad, 1996). No book brings out more how the imagination of the Church is inspired by the imagination of Jesus himself. For a bracing emphasis on the Eucharist and its relationship to Christian hope, three books continue to be influential: Geoffrey Wainwright, *Eucharist and Eschatology* (London: Epworth Press, 1971), Gustave Martelet, *The Risen Christ and the Eucharistic World*, René Hague, trans. (New York: Seabury, 1976), and the Redemptorist, F. X. Durrwell, *L'Eucharistie sacrament pascal* (Paris: Cerf, 1981).

The tradition of the Eastern Churches is well represented in John Zizioulas, *Being As Communion: Studies in Personhood and the Church* (London: Darton, Longman and Todd, 1985) and Boris Bobrinskoy, *The Mystery of the Trinity: Trinitarian Experience and Vision in the Biblical and Patristic Tradition*. Trans. A.P. Gythiel (Crestwood, N.Y.: St. Vladimir's Seminary Press, 1999), each of which has significant sections on the Eucharist.

In a more devotional and mystical key, Michael L. Gaudoin-Parker, *Hymn of Freedom: Celebrating and Living the Eucharist* (Edinburgh: T & T Clark, 1997) merits a mention. For those who have a more philosophical interest, there is—most accessibly—David F. Ford, *Self and Salvation: Being Transformed* (Cambridge: Cambridge University Press, 1999); but among more specialist studies, Jean-Luc Marion, *God Without Being. Hors-Texte*, Thomas A. Carlson, trans., (Chicago: Chicago University Press, 1991) and Catherine Pickstock, *After Writing: On the Liturgical Consummation of Philosophy* (Oxford, U.K., Malden, Mass.: Blackwell, 1997).

It was, I think, Emily Dickinson who wrote, "The possible's slow fuse is lit by the imagination." May it be so in a eucharistic sense, at the turn of the millennium dated from the birth of Jesus of Nazareth two thousand years ago.

TONY KELLY, C.Ss.R.

∽ 1 ∾
THE EUCHARISTIC IMAGINATION

Eucharistic Thinking—and Imagining

Eighteen hundred years ago, Saint Irenaeus of Lyons had to deal with Gnosticism, the heady "new age" spirituality of his day. At that time, he laid down a basic rule that has held true for every age of the Church: "Our way of thinking is attuned to the Eucharist; and the Eucharist, in turn, confirms our way of thinking."[1] Christian thinking—as well as all the theologies that support it—must find in the Eucharist the criterion by which to measure its creative fidelity to tradition. When our way of thinking is attuned to the Eucharist, it is always conscious of much more than can be expressed in either words or thoughts. The eucharistic presence of Christ—incarnate, crucified, and risen—is the focal reality from which we generate our ideas and words and determine the ways in which we conduct our lives. Jesus' "real presence" gives substance and direction to our efforts to understand and express what has been revealed.

The Eucharist, however, confirms our way of thinking and acting only if it is genuinely Christian. To the degree that the faith we profess and the kinds of theology or spirituality we practice resonate with the eucharistic mystery, they are recognized as authentic.

If, therefore, the Eucharist suggests a "way of thinking," it must also be a way of imagining. Because our greatest thoughts take on life from our images, our thinking is embodied in and refreshed by images. The loftiest thinkers, the most brilliant scientists, the most inspired artists: all, in their own unique ways, produce images to communicate what they have explored. In that

1

same way, we will explore what might be called the "eucharistic imagination," a way of thinking and feeling that follows on the special imagination that the Eucharist inspires.

In whatever way eucharistic imagination might be best expressed, it will be intimately related to the imagination of Jesus himself. The Eucharist, in a profound sense, actually clothes us with the imagination of Jesus—the manner in which he imagined God, himself, his mission, and his own ongoing presence in the lives of those who follow him.

The Imagination of the Church

The Eucharist is summit and source of the life of the Church.[2] When it is the "summit," all the activity of the Church is intent on forming the eucharistic community, a "holy communion." As the "source," the Eucharist forms, sustains, and inspires the mission of the Church—and thus that "holy communion" becomes ever larger. In this regard, the Eucharist is not so much a map or blueprint of the Church, but an actual crossing of ways, a gathering and a going out, a communion and a mission, a deeper openness to the grace that has been given, and a thanksgiving, because the divine gift keeps on being given in the present reality of our lives. We not only receive the body and blood of the Lord but also, in the power of his Spirit, lift up our hearts to the loving source from which flow all the gifts of God. For these reasons, we choose the term, *imagination*, thus suggesting something of the many-sided experience that the Eucharist inspires.

The eucharist imagination turns on the great truth and realities of Christian faith: "Christ has died, Christ is risen, Christ will come again." Yet these great truths inspire a new sense of identity. As members of Christ's body and clothed with his imagination, a new sense of community results. In communion, we exist, nurtured by Jesus' body and blood, in the Spirit and imagination of Jesus himself. Not only do we celebrate the truth of the real presence of Jesus in his Incarnation, death, and Resurrection— and not only are we given a new identity and drawn into a new community—but we are compelled, as followers of Christ, to act as he acted. In the conduct of our lives, we are to act with world-transforming energies, with those fruits of the Spirit that Paul lists as "love, joy, peace, patience, kindness, generosity, faithfulness, gentleness, and self-control" (Galatians 5:22–23a). Such energizing gifts are boundless in their scope: "There is no law against such things" (v. 23b). To act in this way is to be possessed and inspired by the Spirit of Jesus himself and to share in his imagination.

In an obvious sense, the ability to imagine is what makes us human. Human beings are not entirely governed by instinct or guided by logic. Rather, it is imagination that gives our lives momentum, direction, and shape. The power of imagination molds our existence into something passionate, defiant, and creative. Above all, this creative capacity of seeing the world "otherwise" is what distinguishes us from the other animals on this planet. Most of all in grief and isolation, in those dark phases of the human journey, imagination comes into its own as a creative energy. It works within the unfinished business of our lives and opens us to forgotten possibilities of grace.

Imagination strains toward life; it knows no other direction. Artists must be patient, playing with many images before their luminous forms emerge; scientists have to experiment with all kinds of formulae and symbolic equations before the moment of insight occurs; perhaps most of all, prisoners, sufferers, and those who are dying would be utterly overwhelmed without the seemingly impractical activity of imagining the world differently—in terms of release, healing, and life in another dimension. It is not unexpected, therefore, that the Church continually reflects on its own sacraments, those symbolic forms of the grace it experiences, in order to reignite its imagination.

Whether we consider the role of imagination theoretically or practically, however, there is risk involved. If we emphasize imagination too much, for example, we may simply feed some kind of fantasy that helps us escape the more real demands of truth and responsibility. It is not uncommon to think that our greatest need is for more information, stronger determination, more efficient management and organization, a more enlightened theology, a keener analysis, more expert strategies—and all this may be true to a certain degree. In fact, there has never been a more analyzed society—nor a more analyzed Church. Dozens of disciplines converge to analyze, diagnose, and plot the path for the future, all following Socrates, who said that the unexamined life was not worth living.

The trouble is that, while our culture "examines" everything, it continues to struggle to find ultimate meaning and value. Why is it, for example, that our analyzing has resulted in nothing more than an increasing sterility and abstraction with regard to what might be termed the flow of real life? Our supposedly cold-eyed analyses seem so oddly disembodied and unconnected to life's direction and promise. We all have been very busy; there are the millions of books, thousands of meetings, and a proliferation of committees—each spawning its own array of subcommittees, each with its minutes, reports, and decisions—resulting in nothing more than another endless round of the same, to set new agendas for a new range of discussions. On it goes.

What we feel most in need of is a master-symbol to grip our imaginations with a sense of our common belonging in the great mystery of life. Without such a focus, our interactions are paper-thin, irritable, and so endlessly wordy. In contrast, imagination is impatient with abstractions because it is intent on life. It is not content to produce thoughts about the world or to fabricate images to adorn that world; rather, it wants to see the world transformed. In a unique way, we will see how the Eucharist is that master-symbol, the one we most need in the midst of the enormously complex world we inhabit.

A future generation, bemused at the libraries of documents bequeathed to them, might well ask, "What were they imagining in all this effort?" More ominously, if those future times should run in the direction of more violence and disillusionment, later generations might ask, "Why did it make so little difference? What did they really want to give us? What sustained them? What taste for life did they share? What hope did they know? What love drove them? How did they imagine life, death, the way we belong together, the inexpressible mystery into which they have now been gathered, leaving only these records left behind?"

Would we not like to respond that the answer lies in the Eucharist we celebrated? Would we not like to ask that we be judged by that—and nothing else? It remains, to connect us to the past and future generations in what really matters, while all else is left to its own fragile fate. But behind any celebration of the Eucharist—past, present, or future—is the work of another imagination, that of Jesus himself.

The Imagination of Jesus

By any showing, Jesus of Nazareth was a man of passionate and inclusive imagination. In the parables he told and in the meals he shared with disciples, sinners, and outcasts, he invited all into his imagination, where he imagined the world other than it was—in contrast to the harsh, God-remote, segregated world the religious and secular authorities of his day had constructed. Jesus' way of imagining the world reached its highest point when, in a final loving meal with those closest to him, he offered himself as one given up for the cause that had occupied his every living moment. In a dramatic gesture, he declared that the bread and wine he shared with those gathered around him were his body, given for the life of the world, and his blood, poured out to seal a new covenant, "poured out for many for the forgiveness of sins" (Matthew 26:28).

As the embodiment of God's love for the world, Jesus identified himself with all whom the idols of his culture—and of every culture—had excluded, demeaned, and killed. Only by sharing in his self-giving love, beyond all violence and revenge, would the murderous heart of the world be disarmed. By entering into his love, the poor in spirit would find that they had entered the Kingdom of God. The meek, by renouncing violence and revenge and by conforming themselves to his way, would be the decisive force in history; they would inherit the earth. To follow him along this path of mercy and forgiveness would mean to find ourselves in a universe of mercy. If, like him, the pure of heart concentrated their lives on God's will and God's reign, they would see God—revealed in the love that Jesus would show. Likewise, the true makers of peace—those who insisted that enemies be reconciled and that the harm we suffer or cause be yielded to a greater healing and to a God-willed unity—would rightly be called God's very own children. Similarly, all who accepted the suffering involved in doing what is right and in witnessing to what is truly good would find themselves anew in God's kingdom. Whatever the bad reputation they might suffer, they would have reason for rejoicing in what was to be revealed (see Matthew 5:3–11).

In Jesus, a new imagination entered the world. By eating his body and drinking his blood through the sharing of the eucharistic bread and wine—in acting as he acted—we are clothed with his imagination.[3]

Four Dimensions of Eucharistic Imagination

In speaking of the eucharistic imagination which Jesus inspires in the Church, four kinds of imagination are implied or, if you like, a Spirit-inspired imagination unfolds in four dimensions.

First, there is the imagination of God. In giving us his Son, the Father has given us an image of himself: "He is the image of the invisible God" (Colossians 1:15) to such a degree that in him "the fullness of God was pleased to dwell" (v. 19) as the source of peace and universal reconciliation. The "mystery that had been hidden throughout the ages and generations" (v. 26) has now been made known. Christ, as the image of God, is the communication of the divine imagination to those who are open to it: "his saints" (v. 26). Believers have been chosen to witness to "how great among the [nations] are the riches of the glory of this mystery, which is Christ in you, the hope of glory" (v. 27).

Next, there is the imagination of Jesus himself. He expressed what he was and wanted to mean to his disciples when he "took a loaf of bread, and when he had given thanks, he broke it and said, 'This is my body that is for you. Do this in remembrance of me.' In the same way he took the cup…'This cup is the new covenant in my blood. Do this…in remembrance of me' " (1 Corinthians 11:23–25).

From his imagination arises the third imagination, that of the Church. By obeying the Lord's command to remember him in this way, the Church as God's people and Christ's Body actively imagines the great mystery on which its faith and hope depend: "For as often as you eat this bread and drink the cup, you proclaim the Lord's death until he comes" (1 Corinthians 11:26). The eucharistic liturgy, following the words of Vatican II already quoted, is "the summit and source of the Church's life"—and imagination. By repeatedly refreshing its imagination through the celebration of the Eucharist, the Church is constantly renewed in its sense of "what no eye has seen, nor ear heard, / nor the human heart conceived / [concerning all that] God has prepared for those who love him" (1 Corinthians 2:9).

Finally, the fourth mode of imagination relates to the previous three: the imagination of God, the imagination of Jesus, and the imagination of the Church. It expresses the manner in which each of us, and the communities to which we belong, exercises a eucharistic imagination in the conduct of our own lives. The Holy Spirit inspires us to make our own the imagination of the Church, to clothe ourselves with the imagination of Jesus himself, and so to enter into God's own imagination of ourselves and our world.

This emphasis on the imaginative aspect of the Eucharist in no sense obscures or downplays the real "presence" of Christ to the Church realized in the transformed bread and wine. Because that objective presence remains central and fundamental, it has consequences for the imaginative life of faith. If we are to fully appreciate Christ's real living presence to us, we must enter into his imagination. To receive his body and blood, to breathe his Spirit, is to allow our imagination to be converted to his way of imagining himself and his relationship to his disciples.

Paul's words to that early community at Philippi suggest the density of eucharistic imagination. Some of these early Christians were evidently lacking a Christlike imagination in their dealings with one another:

> Be of the same mind, having the same love, being in full accord and of one mind. Do nothing from selfish ambition or conceit, but in humility regard others as better than yourselves. Let each of you look not to your own interests, but to the interests of others. Let the same mind be in you that was in Christ Jesus (Philippians 2:2–5).

The apostle then goes on to give his version of an early Christian hymn celebrating the selfless love of Christ (see vv. 6–11) as he "emptied himself, / taking the form of a slave" (v. 7). The way Jesus imagined himself in his relationship with the Father and to all he came to save was startlingly different from the world's way of imagining both God and human dignity: "He humbled himself / and became obedient to the point of death— / even death on a cross" (v. 8). Yet, it is his way that God has vindicated, the way of humble self-giving love: "Therefore God has highly exalted him" (v. 9). We suggest, then, that through the Eucharist we make our own the imagination that guided Jesus along the path of self-emptying love that led to his glorification and our salvation. Let the same mind, the same imagination, be in us that was in Christ Jesus. By being baptized "into Christ" and, consequently, by participating in the Eucharist, we have "clothed" ourselves with Christ (see Galatians 3:27). One result of this is to be clothed with his imagination.

To give another example: At Pentecost, Peter cited the words of the prophet Joel to evoke the energy and wonder of the new life that the Spirit would bring. A new imagination, inspired by the Spirit Jesus sends from the Father, was unfolding. The young would see visions and the old would dream dreams beyond anything a dispirited, lost world could imagine. But such a conviction does not imply an otherworldly life of ecstatic rapture, religious enthusiasm, or an escape from the world. Rather, it is concerned with transforming the world. The movement of the Spirit brings us back to earth as we celebrate the Eucharist. It gives shape and substance to a new world of relationships. The visions and dreams that were foretold are nothing less than a participating in the eucharistic imagination of Jesus himself. By eating his body and drinking his blood, the Church is continually revitalized in the imagination that inspires its life and mission.

Such a way of imagining is, indeed, always unsettling. It disturbs every fantasy world that our human culture has ever tended to create. To the degree we are trapped in the flat, driven world of our obsessions, the Eucharist appears, not as giving us his real presence, but as something empty, tasteless, and useless, unrelated to what we are and need to be. On the other hand, to the degree his eucharistic presence is the summit and source of our lives, we are living from an inexhaustible abundance, the energies of life filled with the power of love and the joy of the resurrection. A seismic disturbance takes place in the grim, flinty patterns of the ways we relate to one another, and upsets the balance of the cold-eyed justice that structures our dealings. That cool logic that is suspicious of the power of feeling, and that routine religion that cannot conceive of any human passion on the part of God: Both suffer a shock when confronted with the flesh and blood of Christ in the Eucharist. Our hearts, too, like the hearts of the disciples at Emmaus, begin to burn within us (see Luke 24:32), as we sense life anew and begin to feel how we are meant to belong together. The sickly constitution of our culture is offered its most healthy food, and the infusion of such blood enters into its anaemic system. This holy communion, built on selfless love, challenged the habitual self-serving patterns of life—and all our subtle strategies of image-making are torn open by this imagination.

Reality: Virtual—And Otherwise

Today we are familiar with those wonderful artificially created images that are termed "virtual reality"—a certain kind of reality that aims to simulate the real thing. Training in a flight simulator, for example, helps pilots prepare for the actual experience of landing an aircraft or handling an emergency. Or the wizardry of virtual reality may be used simply for the sake of a computer game. There is a thrill, for example, in imagining ourselves driving a racing car or outwitting a monster.

The Eucharist, however, is not a virtual reality of this kind. Rather, it is a Spirit-inspired form of actual reality that draws us out of all the virtual realities our culture or society offers. The Eucharist does not simply feed our imaginations with alternative images; it offers the "real food and real drink" of eternal life. It gives the truth that will make us free (see John 8:32). In its divinely charged reality, the Eucharist sustains a way of realistically imagining God, ourselves, and our world in the light of the faith, hope, and love that has been breathed into us.

Fundamentally, the Eucharist invites us to bring together what we so often keep apart: our ways of imagining God, ourselves, our relations with others, and the universe itself. It does not take us out of the real world, but into it. It causes us to "re-member," to bring together, our fractured experience on all these levels, by joining us to Christ's Body and inviting us into his imagination.

In defiant contrast to the world of "image making," the eucharistic imagination opens our experience to a universe of grace and a universe of givers. We live in time, and experience its ambiguities with thanksgiving and hope, moving forward in the depths of the imagination that the Spirit inspires.

Other Imaginations

In the meantime, other imaginations are at work as well—at odds, actually, with the eucharistic imagination, and yet impelling toward it. There is, after all, something to learn from the great atheists of our time—those "masters of suspicion" such as Marx, Freud, and Nietzsche who have pricked the balloon of religious fantasy. Each in his own way has unwittingly jolted us out of frozen images into a more wholesome and compassionate imagining. Let me try to express this point in the briefest possible way.[4]

Marx, for instance, posed a deep challenge to the religious and philosophical foundations of capitalism. After him, any faith that is unrelated to the dispossessed of one's world is inherently suspect. As has often been pointed out, Marx's questioning of God makes Christians expose themselves to the "dangerous memory" of Jesus who was executed as a criminal for his solidarity with the poor and the outcast in the society of that time. Because remembering his death means an examination of our conscience, a genuine eucharistic imagination must include an awareness of the global dimensions of poverty and injustice: "As often as you did it…" (see Matthew 25:31–46). Paradoxically, under the leadership of recent popes and the great pastoral bishops of the Third World such as Oscar Romero and Helder Camara, the Church has become the main carrier of Marx's original inspiration, even though Marxism as a system of repressive government has failed. In allowing the Eucharist to nourish our social conscience more critically, we will be better prepared to hear John's words: "Little children, keep yourselves from idols" (1 John 5:21)—especially now that the real "opium of the people" has been more clearly identified not as religion, as Marx thought, but as the addictive consumerism of our day.

Similarly, there is the challenge of Freud. In his delving into the inarticulate and unexpressed emotional life of his patients, he concluded that religion was the projection of the immature. He saw it simply as a neurotic refusal in the face of the tough business of personal responsibility. To Freud, the religious were essentially infantile, people who displaced their responsibility into a myth of God fabricated as the ultimate "father image." As a result, any religious tradition must show that it is able to live with Freud's critique and examine its own conscience. Christian believers must be prepared, therefore, to ask themselves, *Is the whole panoply of our religious lives designed as a refuge for the infantile and immature, for those refusing the harsh realism of life and death?* Today, the Freudian movement has become established as a profession, even an industry. It does, however, exhibit its own limitations: Therapists, for example, "free" their clients to conform to diseased and inhuman cultural forms in which more than sexuality is repressed and where Spirit has become an extinct dimension. Fortunately, the question has been posed, and it is unwise for anyone concerned with the spiritual in our culture to deny its challenge. By freeing religious faith from infantile fantasy, the Freudian critique can release the creative potential of religious imagination to face the psychic terrors involved in being a mortal human being—and thereby find the courage to live life as an original gift.

Again, we are challenged with the issue of a genuine eucharistic imagination: As we celebrate the death of the Lord until he comes, as we reach out to others in obedience to the new commandment, we leave behind a private fantasy world. In this, our motivation is not consolation for ourselves, but the values of a realistic human community: forgiveness, compassion for the suffering, joy in the success of others, hope for all, and a humble confession of our sinfulness. The Eucharist contests the bias of individual fantasy by drawing us into the public imagination of the Church, thereby guiding our lives, in the midst of the pain, risk, and ambiguities inherent in our world, along the long path of selfless love and goodness.

Psychotherapists have long been familiar with the Babel of voices and fixations that haunt the disturbed mind, and commentators on modern culture often point to consumerism as a mask for the pervasive depression and meaninglessness that plague populations around the world. The tragedy of all this is that people are individuals in a society made up of so many depressingly private worlds. In such a social reality, dominated by feelings of fear, anger, and worthlessness, the shared imagination freezes, and we can't imagine ourselves differently. Isolation and a sense of hopelessness cut us off from the real world of relationship and responsibility. Our culture, cut off from anything outside itself, works to confirm our sense of rootlessness and apathy.

In this regard, the eucharistic imagination heals the cultural sickness that feeds on its own fantasies. It draws us out of ourselves and our failures into an infinitely larger world of belonging. For to celebrate the Eucharist is to enter into a universe of love and intimate relationships with God, with one another, and with the universe itself. When we begin to imagine ourselves and our world in the light of the Eucharist, Christ's living presence disturbs the fantasies of depressive despair with the energies of hope. If before, we could only think of ourselves and our depressed state, now the Eucharist invites us into the way of love and compassion for others with whom we are united. Isolation gives way to a great communion of life where thanksgiving and praise take us into a universe in which God's love has been revealed. The inevitable suffering involved in every human life is made productive by uniting us to the passion of Jesus himself.

Finally—and perhaps most important to our contemporary literary culture—there is Nietzsche. Although his name has been rendered ambiguous by the Nazi use of his myth of the "superman," his rage was especially directed against what he understood as the religious divinization of the antihuman. To his mind, traditional Christian culture had exalted passivity and self-abnegation in a mean-spirited suspicion of the human in the name of religion.

Christianity is a servile kind of faith whose idea of God degenerates into the contradiction of life; instead of being its transfiguration and eternal "Yes!" God is the declaration of war against life, against nature, against the will to live! God—the formula for every slander against this world, for every lie about the beyond, God the deification of nothingness, the will to nothingness pronounced holy.[5]

It is not difficult to find in oneself a sympathetic response to what Nietzsche was getting at. When religious people protest against the godlessness of the world, they too often sound as though they are turning against humanity itself. They may talk about salvation but, as Nietzsche remarked on one occasion, they don't look saved! But, of course, that is not the whole story—neither then nor now. Nietzsche could hardly have foreseen the time when the champions of "transcendent humanism" would be popes, and that Vatican II would begin its "Pastoral Constitution on the Church in the Modern World" (*Gaudium et Spes*) with the words:

The joy and hope, the grief and anguish of the [people] of our time, especially of those who are poor or afflicted in any way, are the joy and hope, the grief and anguish of the followers of Christ as well. Nothing that is genuinely human fails to find an echo in their hearts....

More generally, the main protesters on behalf of a more human and just way of life would be activist Christians contesting the increasingly flat and fragmented world that has come into being. Yet Nietzsche's challenge remains—to unsettle any merely cultural form of Christianity that has lost its power to imagine the world otherwise.

More particularly, Nietzsche provokes us into entering into the eucharistic imagination more creatively. The truth that saves and frees is not an disembodied abstraction; rather, it is expressed in the flesh and blood of our human history. It grapples with the terrible realities of evil and suffering while, at the same time, celebrating the inexhaustible gift of God's love in Christ. For Christians, it is not merely a matter of having some new mysterious information, but of being transformed by a truth that is to be lived and assimilated and imagined, making them see everything differently—the whole of creation, blessed, healed, and made open to its ultimate transformation. The bread and wine of our daily lives is transformed into the gift of Christ's body and blood. The truth is food and drink, communion in the love-life of God's own trinitarian being.

The Modern World: A Failure of Imagination?

The modern world is an enormous bundle of success and failure. Enlightenment rationalism succeeded in liberating the human mind from many forms of dehumanizing dependence, but the price has been great. For such independence was so highly prized that any dependence on God has become all but impossible to express. To that all-controlling rationalist world, God was understood to be a rival to the human. Further, human independence was so absolutized that it actually lost its connection with nature. In the bleak technological world of its making, the human mind has become a stranger to itself, a ghost haunting a devastated planet. Thus human beings, too, have lost their place. The influential American Passionist visionary, Tom Berry, catches the dimensions of the problem we are struggling with. In reference to the last two hundred years of Western history, he writes:

> During this period the human mind lived in the narrowest bonds it has ever experienced. The vast mythic, visionary, symbolic world with its all-pervasive numinous qualities was lost. Because of this loss, humanity made its terrifying assault upon the earth with an irrationality that is stunning in enormity while we were being assured that this was the way to a better, more humane, more reasonable world.[6]

With such stunting of imagination, human freedoms have thus become cramped into the constraints of big government and mass control. Sadly, such a wasted inner environment is hard put to recognize the devastation of the outer environment. Even if something like a deathbed conversion is taking place, the illness has not be cured.

Today, the cultivation of a deeply, passionately eucharistic imagination is crucial. It must be allowed to guide the way we think and act and relate to one another in the light of God. The Church is not enclosed in an economy of scarcity; rather, its resources are continuously renewable. While grace keeps on being grace, the life-giving love of God is never exhausted. While calling into question what has gone so terrifyingly wrong, it invites the imagination to expand in a universe of grace. In a special sense, the Eucharist is the primary instance of "imagination as the irrepressible revolutionist" (Wallace Stevens). Most of all, such imagination will resist that modern kind of corrosive pessimism that leads to paralysis and depression rather than to the release of creative energies. The limitless capacity of the Holy Spirit surprises every age with the unforeseeably new. In this world of mustard seeds, the tree of the kingdom is nurtured by the imagination that the Eucharist inspires. It gathers us in to share the one bread of life—"our daily bread," a phrase which might be more accurately translated as "the bread that really matters."[7] Nourished by such bread, the imagination is set free, as when, in the words of Shakespeare, it "bodies forth / the forms of things unknown... /

turns them into shapes, and give to airy nothing / A local habitation and a name."[8] The Eucharist, celebrated in the daily round of the Church's life, provokes a profound reimagining of the world we have made in the light of what God intends it to be.

∾ 2 ∾
PAUL'S STRUGGLING IMAGINATION

(1 and 2 Corinthians)

I n commending a eucharistic imagination, we naturally take into account a number of key references to the Eucharist in the New Testament. The imposing resources of current biblical scholarship, of course, are essential in such a project. Yet, from the perspective adopted here, there is room for a quiet movement in another direction. It is not so much that the Eucharist is found "in" the Scriptures, but that the meaning of the Scriptures is found "in" the Eucharist as it is celebrated in the daily life of the Church. For the sacrament of Christ's self-giving love interprets and makes present for the community the reality to which the Scriptures witness. Indeed, it is most probable that all the writings of the New Testament were designed to be read in a eucharistic setting and, in some explicit cases, contained the homilies and hymns that actually occurred in the eucharistic liturgy. I do not think, therefore, that it is a concession to uncritical piety to emphasize eucharistic imagination as an essential dimension of biblical exegesis. The Bible is the book of the Church's faith; and the Eucharist, as the summit and source of the life of the Church, remains a compact, often tacit, measure of what the words of Scripture intend to communicate.

The Eucharist, celebrated in the various contexts of the Church's journey through history, is saturated with the meaning of the mysteries of faith. Christ is present to believers, and believers are present to Christ and to one another in a way that actualizes the meaning of Scripture and makes it a living reality. This is not to suggest that all the patient labor of biblical scholarship is of no account; merely, that the eucharistic imagination is, on its own level, essential for a lived sense of what the word of Scripture is witness to. The biblical Word completes itself in the sacrament, and the sacrament is the real presence of the Christ to whom the inspired writers have witnessed.

The Eucharist at Corinth

The various versions of the Eucharist found in the gospels—each with its own emphasis—show how the early Christian communities "did this in memory of him" and clothed themselves with his imagination. Their living union with the risen Lord, their memory of what he had bequeathed to them the night before he died, and the treasured recollections of all that he had done and said and suffered made this imagination an ever productive force in the life of faith. Take, for example, the earliest references to the Eucharist in First Corinthians (written possibly twenty years before the gospels, and within twenty-five years of the Crucifixion). If the Corinthians had not misbehaved in a scandalous and disorderly manner, it is possible that Paul would not have mentioned the Eucharist at all. But it was, in fact, so much part of his imagination that it was the reality to which he turned to set his wayward Corinthian disciples along the right path.

Responsible Freedom

Some of the disciples in Corinth, apparently intoxicated by their new sense of Christian freedom, were giving scandal by eating food that had been sacrificed to idols. They were giving free reign to their imagination based exclusively on their sense of individual freedom. After all, understanding that pagan idols were nothing, they could see no harm in availing themselves of this cut-price meat, a comparatively rare commodity in their situation. If, they reasoned, any of their number were scandalized by this, it was simply a sign of immaturity.

But there are other idols that are far more insidious, fabricated by imagining the grace of God or salvation in Christ apart from the demands of the self-giving love represented by the cross. Freedom in Christ was, indeed, a precious gift, but it, too, had to be imagined according to the pattern of Jesus' self-sacrificing love. The Israelites of old, having turned aside from the demands inherent in their unique relationship to God, had lapsed into idolatry of self-indulgence (see 1 Corinthians 10:6–11). The same problem was now confronting the believers in Corinth: "Therefore, my dear friends, flee from the worship of idols. I speak as to sensible people; judge for yourselves what I say" (vv. 14–15). Paul recalls these "sensible people" to an authentic eucharistic imagination:

> The cup of blessing that we bless, is it not a sharing in the blood of Christ? The bread that we break, is it not a sharing in the body of Christ? Because there is one bread, we who are many are one body, for we all partake of the one bread (vv. 16–17).

Communion in the body and blood of Christ is the decisive principle, and anything that undermines this principle is the sign of a contrary imagination at work: "You cannot drink the cup of the Lord and the cup of demons. You cannot partake of the table of the Lord and the table of demons" (v. 21). Even if, through the grace of Christian liberty, "all things are lawful" (v. 23), the decisive element in Christian imagination and conduct is what is "beneficial," and what "builds up" (v. 23). If Paul's hearers are to live by recollecting what Jesus has done, and so share in his imagination—"Do not seek your own advantage, but that of the other" (v. 24)—then those united to Christ cannot imagine themselves independently of their loving responsibility to the whole community—"the other's conscience, not your own" (v. 29). Paul himself is so imbued with the imagination of Jesus that he can exhort his hearers to follow his own example: "…just as I try to please everyone in everything I do, not seeking my own advantage, but that of many, so that they may be saved. Be imitators of me, as I am of Christ" (1 Corinthians 10:33—11:1).

Paul's eucharistic imagination, as it comes suddenly into play, expresses an intense concern for the building up of the community as a realistic communion in Christ. Even if, all things being equal, eating temple meat is legitimate, that freedom must be foregone for the sake of unity in Christ. It is not a matter of celebrating only the presence of Christ, but of entering into his imagination and of sharing in his self-giving love. A eucharistic imagination sees everything differently.

An Inclusive Imagination

Another "happy fault" of the Corinthians gives Paul further occasion to drive home the essential meaning of the Eucharist—that concerning the arrogant and selfish behavior of well-off people at the meals during which the Eucharist was celebrated. It seems the poor were left feeling that they were alien intruders, that they could share the Eucharist with their privileged brothers and sisters, but not much else. The Christian Corinthian meetings had become occasions of division:

> Now in the following instructions I do not commend you, because when you come together it is not for the better but for the worse. For, to begin with, when you come together as a church, I hear that there are divisions among you; and to some extent I believe it. Indeed, there have to be factions among you, for only so will it become clear who among you are genuine (1 Corinthians 11:17–19).

Any time Christians gather for the Eucharist, of course, the situation is never entirely innocent. To some extent, we are all a scandal to one another, even if unwittingly. The other ways we have nourished our lives, the other food we have fed on—anything the supermarket of the seven deadly sins might have abundantly supplied—has left its mark. Less graphically, we each come to the celebration in need of forgiveness and reconciliation, perhaps in ways we can hardly name.

When we look around at the congregation or the community, resentful of having dragged ourselves away from more important things or more interesting people, we are often inclined to ask, "What on earth am I going to get out of this? Why am I here?" Such questioning catches us out, for it arises from a bias against what the Eucharist should mean for us. We are thus confronted with a choice: Is the Eucharist the genuine expression of my life? Is this where I belong? Is this what I really want to do? Is this what I mean by my life? Such questions allow us to see how the "factions" to which we implicitly belong tend to make us anti-Eucharist. To this degree, we are set against the Eucharist's fullest meaning, unready to accept the gift and demands of our union in Christ.

Here, Paul's words hit the point. After referring to the reports he has heard about divisions among the Corinthians, he goes on to say: "Indeed, there have to be factions among you, for only so will it become clear who among you are genuine" (1 Corinthians 11:19). The Eucharist always demands a decision—not dramatic usually, but enough to cause us to recommit ourselves to Christ, to his Church, and to the real people of this community. In other words, union with Christ and communion with one another must be realized by countering the bias and distraction that tend to take us in different directions. Gathering for the Eucharist happens in the teeth of conflicts and factions that are, practically speaking, always present. There is always a reason to see the Eucharist as unreal. The challenge is to let its reality find us out, invite us into a new imagination, in contrast to the "unreality" that has structured our lives. Paul unmasks the sorry situation which, in different ways, affects the Church in every age:

When you come together, it is not really to eat the Lord's supper. For when the time comes to eat, each of you goes ahead with your own supper, and one goes hungry and another becomes drunk. What! Do you not have homes to eat and drink in? Or do you show contempt for the church of God and humiliate those who have nothing? (vv. 20–22).

If there is no genuine appreciation of what is celebrated and shared, other motives take over. For some, in this situation in the early Church, the eucharistic gathering had become a mere social event, a convivial meeting with like-minded friends and families. No doubt, there was an atmosphere of rejoicing in what was taken to be the freedom and joy of the Gospel—for the Lord had risen and the Spirit had been poured out. But without a realistic focus in the self-giving love of Christ, the general enthusiasm tended toward amnesia with regard to what the Eucharist was meant to communicate. Some of the more socially privileged were, in fact, forgetting what they had most reason to remember, and this was playing false to the character of the love that had been shown them. Unlike God, unlike Christ, they were making themselves into an elite group that excluded the poorer, the weaker, those they considered to be unworthy of belonging:

> Consider your own call, brothers and sisters: not many of you were wise by human standards, not many were powerful, not many were of noble birth. But God chose what is foolish in the world to shame the wise; God chose what is weak in the world to shame the strong; God chose what is low and despised in the world, the things that are not, to reduce to nothing the things that are, so that no one might boast in the presence of God (1 Corinthians 1:26–29).

In this case, the "wise," the "powerful," the "noble," the self-sufficient elements of the community, needed to allow themselves to be "shamed" into a deeper sense of all-inclusive love. They were inverting God's scale of preference, and inventing for themselves a kind of fellowship that owed nothing to the gospel. Their freedom in Christ, tending toward a self-gratifying escape from responsibility for the less privileged, had to become a loving concern for them. Christ is really present in the whole body of his members as they live out the demands of an all-inclusive compassionate love:

> In this matter I do not commend you! For I received from the Lord what I also handed on to you, that the Lord Jesus on the night when he was betrayed took a loaf of bread, and when he had given thanks, he broke it and said, "This is my body that is for you. Do this in remembrance of me." In the same way, he took the cup also, after supper, saying, "This cup is the new covenant in my blood. Do this, as often as you drink it, in remembrance of me." For as often as you eat this bread and drink the cup, you proclaim the Lord's death until he comes (1 Corinthians 11:22–26).

In these words, Paul recalls the community to what is at stake. The Eucharist implies both recalling the tradition that he received and handed on, and entering into its living meaning. He invites his readers into the imagination of Jesus himself. For the Lord, in the face of betrayal, condemnation, and death, had taken the bread and wine and offered it to his disciples as the symbols of his total self-gift—"my body that is for you" and his blood poured out in "the new covenant." Believers are to "remember" him by doing as he has done, not only by eating the bread and drinking the wine but also by participating actively in what is signified, namely, Christ himself, in his self-giving love. His body has been given and his blood shed in order to be sustenance and form of the Christian community in its journey through time. To "proclaim the death of the Lord until he comes" is to surrender to the demands of a love that ever goes beyond itself for others, even to the point of death. Though life must go on in this time of waiting and hope, when no love is ever perfect and no community is ever ideal, the Lord will come as the fulfillment and vindication of the selfless love to which we are called. To be united with him and in communion with others demands continual discernment:

> Whoever, therefore, eats the bread or drinks the cup of the Lord in an unworthy manner will be answerable for the body and blood of the Lord. Examine yourselves, and only then eat of the bread and drink of the cup. For all who eat and drink without discerning the body, eat and drink judgment against themselves. For this reason, many of you are weak and ill, and some have died. But if we judged ourselves, we would not be judged. But when we are judged by the Lord, we are disciplined so that we may not be condemned along with the world (vv. 27–32).

To hope for the coming of the Lord while failing to practice the love that the Eucharist embodies is to lay oneself open to his coming as judgment of condemnation. Celebrating the Eucharist unworthily is linked to showing "contempt for the Church of God and [humiliating] those who have nothing" (v. 22). Unworthy eating and drinking is to be unmindful of the Eucharist as the realization of love in our midst. To the degree, as individuals or communities, we live such a contradiction, we excommunicate ourselves from the "holy communion" that Jesus intends. Hence, a deep examination of conscience is always necessary, lest we use the Eucharist to bolster our own prejudices and to harden the ruts of loveless inaction in which selfishness tends to settle. If Socrates declared that the unexamined life was not worth living, the Eucharist demands that we examine our lives to bring them into line with what we celebrate. If we are to share in the generosity of the giver, our imaginations must catch up with the gift that has been given. To celebrate the Eucharist in an unexamined manner, therefore, can lead to a scandal in the life of the community. What is meant to unite across all social boundaries is made into an occasion in which social divisions are accentuated. As a result, the holiest and most loving act is being violently subverted.

Little wonder, then, to Paul's mind, this kind of scandalous celebration of the Eucharist brings about a death-dealing conflict in the community. It makes people sick and incapable of digesting the rich food of love and enduring life. Yet, if we come to the Eucharist attentive to its deepest meaning, this violent situation will be avoided. The eucharistic reality—"proclaiming the death of the Lord until he comes"—will affirm rather than condemn what we are. We will be living the truth about ourselves and God, even though it is yet to be fully revealed. It will find us in a state of conversion, in an openness to the Lord materialized in the responsible love for our fellow members in the Body of Christ. By exposing ourselves to the coming reality of Christ, we distance ourselves, step by step, from the ways of the world that have no future: violence, selfishness, greed, divisions, and segregations that lead nowhere. The apostle goes on:

So then, my brothers and sisters, when you come together to eat, wait for one another. If you are hungry, eat at home, so that when you come together, it will not be for your condemnation (vv. 33–34).

What Paul demands here is a patience and care with regard to the real people who make up the community. Insensitivity to others must yield to concern not to exclude, or give the impression of excluding, those whom Christ has already included in his love. What we do must be in remembrance of him, with a vivid sense of his self-sacrifice for all. To put it most bluntly, it so easy to forget "what it's all about." If the Eucharist is regarded merely as a community celebration but without a care for the forgotten or the excluded, it is in danger of being unreal and dishonest. Even to think of it as a means of obtaining the real presence of Jesus among us, but without the disposition to enter into his heart and imagination, jeopardizes the sense of outreaching community it is meant to signify and bring about.

The Imagination of Love

The apostle's spirited reaction to the various scandals bedeviling the divided Corinthian community climaxes in his hymn to Christian love. The imagination of Christ and the eucharistic imagination of the community are both judged according to the criteria of self-forgetful love:

> Love is patient; love is kind; love is not envious or boastful or arrogant or rude. It does not insist on its own way; it is not irritable or resentful; it does not rejoice in wrongdoing, but rejoices in the truth. It bears all things, believes all things, hopes all things, endures all things. Love never ends (1 Corinthians 13:4–8).

The Lord's command, "Do this in memory of me," places those who gather to celebrate the Eucharist always in a state of apprenticeship. What he commands us is not just to gather to share food—even if such a sharing presupposes sharing on the basic level of our humanity. Certainly it requires some readiness to share, some sense of belonging together in reconciliation and justice and, of course, some skill in preparing the food and arranging a meal. Moreover, since it is a liturgical act, the various skills in language, gesture, art, and ritual are presupposed.

But the *this* that is to be performed in his memory is more. It strikes deeper. What is at stake is conforming our lives and conduct to the self-giving love that characterizes Christ's relationship to us. His love inspired the surrender of his whole being—in his body and blood, in his life, death, and resurrection—for the sake of the world's reconciliation to God. And so "the love of Christ urges us on....And he died for all, so that those who live might live no longer for themselves, but for him who died and was raised for them" (2 Corinthians 5:14–15).

In his mission of reconciliation, Christ's love was unreserved. Since it went to the limit of dying for us, we are to proclaim "the death of the Lord until he comes." The excess of love, going beyond all boundaries and divisions, is fundamental to the eucharistic imagination, leaving us always in a state of apprenticeship. We will never be eucharistically authentic until our own love, for our neighbor and the world itself, has gone to the end, by giving over our lives to God's saving purpose. In hope and patience we must bear with the whole agonized, unfinished complexity of the world and its history, and of each one of us as participants within the world. In the patience that finds its hope only in the coming of the Lord, we remember his cross and resurrection as the defining moment of what love for God and the world truly means, even if its fullness is not yet experienced. Because the love of Christ ever surpasses our capacities to realize it, we only move toward it, in waiting, in patience, and in hope—"until he comes." The love of Christ simply cannot be possessed or contained within the dimensions of the present.

Still, it is not as though we are left merely reaching back in memory to what was once given, or endlessly deferring to some unknown future. Rather, we are already his body. Already we share the bread of life and drink the cup of salvation. Already we take and eat what has been given beyond human limits. His unlimited gift already received, already our sustenance and communion, takes us to the outermost limit at which we touch on what is to come. We live beyond ourselves in the energies and sustenance that flow from Christ's love, drawn out of any ambiguous present into a patient hope for the salvation of the entire world. Amateurs, apprentices, and pilgrims though we are in our capacity to appreciate the dimensions of what God has prepared for those who love him (see 1 Corinthians 2:9), the Eucharist leads us to a deep hearing of Paul's words, this time as he addresses the Romans:

> Therefore, since we are justified by faith, we have peace with
> God through our Lord Jesus Christ, through whom we have
> obtained access to this grace in which we stand; and we boast

in our hope of sharing the glory of God. And not only that, but we also boast in our sufferings, knowing that suffering produces endurance, and endurance produces character, and character produces hope, and hope does not disappoint us, because God's love has been poured into our hearts through the Holy Spirit that has been given to us (Romans 5:1–5).

In its celebration of the Eucharist, the community of faith has "peace with God," since already it enjoys the gift of an intimate and unbreakable relationship with God in Christ. Nothing "in all creation will be able to separate us from the love of God in Christ Jesus our Lord" (Romans 8:39). God's love for us has made our destiny secure—in nothing less than sharing in the divine glory. But that love, disturbing the limited scope of our individual lives and the social boundaries that often violently separate us from others, causes its own kind of suffering. When God's love has entered the world, it leaves us and our world deeply disturbed, radically unfinished, at a distance from our final destiny. For love cannot rest content with anything less than the complete transformation of the world. It results in its own sharp-edged sufferings caused by the needs of others, by the burden of our own responsibilities and, above all, by the apparent weakness and folly of what the Eucharist represents—the self-giving love of the cross of Christ. Tempted to impatience in the face of the long haul of a love that must keep reaching beyond itself, we must have time for all—in a way that models itself on the patience of God's providence for all—including ourselves, in our failures, hesitations, confusions, and wasted opportunities. The Eucharist is peace, but it is also suffering. Still, through its daily celebration, endurance grows and we enter into the patience of God—and with that, we are slowly conformed to the self-giving character of Christ himself. Clothed with the mind and imagination of Christ, hope emerges. The Eucharist is a refusal to settle for defeat and despair. In memory of him, conscious of the excess of the love of Christ, it waits for his return. This hope is on sure ground, because already Christ nourishes us with his flesh and blood, and breathes his Spirit into his whole Body, the Holy Spirit who pours into our hearts the love of God in a unfailing stream of the gifts.

Saint Augustine, pondering the passages we have treated on

the previous pages, offers a striking conclusion to what we have been suggesting:

> If you wish, then, to understand the Body of Christ, listen to the Apostle as he says to the faithful, "You are the Body of Christ and his members" (1 Corinthians 12:27). If, therefore, you are the Body of Christ and his members, your mystery has been placed on the Lord's table, you receive your mystery. You reply "Amen" to that which you are, and by replying you consent. For you hear, "The Body of Christ," and you reply "Amen." Be a member of the Body of Christ so that your "Amen" may be true.[1]

ᴔ 3 ᴕ
ON THE WAY TO EMMAUS
(Luke 24:13-35)

For the two early disciples, and for those who will join them in successive generations in "the breaking of the bread," the road to Emmaus is a movement toward conversion and the awakening of the eucharistic imagination.

An Unpromising Situation

The scene opens with two disciples as they leave Jerusalem on that first Easter Sunday—the day that the whole Gospel had been moving toward (see Luke 24:13-36). In fact, the two disciples are leaving behind a scene of utter confusion that had resulted from the women's disconcerting account of what they had witnessed at the tomb: the stone had been rolled back and the tomb was found empty. Two light-clad figures had confronted the women with a bewildering question and an amazing statement: "Why do you look for the living among the dead? He is not here, but has risen" (v. 5). What had happened was exactly what Jesus had foretold (see vv. 6-7). But when these first witnesses reported all this to the apostles and the rest of the disciples, they were greeted with incredulity. Still, Peter had gone to check for himself, only to find that, indeed, the grave-clothes lay in an empty tomb. He went back amazed (see v. 12).

What had really happened? That was the question obviously on the mind of the two travelers. With the women so convinced, the disciples so unimpressed, and Peter just thunderstruck by the whole business, these two disciples were simply at a loss. Certainly nothing that came up in their conversation inclined them to turn around and return to the city. Rather, they felt let down by this man who had inspired in them wondrous feelings of hope and expectation. They had been lifted up to the heights only—with his condemnation and death—to come crashing down to earth. But now, well...all that was best left behind. The two simply needed to make the journey *away* from Jerusalem—a place that meant only crushing disappointment and defeat. Jerusalem, the Holy City: they had thought of it as the hub of salvation, the place where the mission of Jesus would be completed. From there his followers were to set out to save the world. Now, given recent events, the disappointed disciples were headed elsewhere, putting it all behind them in search of a peace undisturbed by what had become so devastatingly out of control.

Imagination Stirs

But then, another story begins to be told, and another imagination stirs: Jesus himself comes near and goes with the two, but their eyes are kept from recognizing him (see v. 16). What was happening was beyond both their sight and imagination, yet Jesus' question makes it clear that he wishes to be part of their conversation. He invites the two to rehearse what they had been speaking about: "What are you discussing with each other while you walk along?" (v. 17). At this point—on the far side of a sadness that could hardly be shared—their new companion seems more a stranger than any stranger in town, and they are stopped in their tracks. One of them, Cleopas, asks, "Are you the only stranger in Jerusalem who does not know the things that have taken place there in these days?" (v. 18). In response, Jesus asks, "What things?" (v. 19). He is not feigning ignorance but rather inviting his fellow travelers to go over everything again in such a way that it will begin to include what they had been leaving out—his continuing presence with them on this journey. In this way, their memory will arrive at a larger remembering.

And so, they tell their story, one that, indeed, tells of "the things about Jesus of Nazareth"—a mighty prophet, handed over to the chief priests and leaders, how he was condemned, and crucified; the reports of the empty tomb and the vision of angels (see vv. 19–24). But the two travelers' account of events seems to collapse in on itself. Their point of reference ceases to be Jesus himself and turns, instead to be a story about themselves and the limits of the imagination that they had brought to the events that had taken place: "*our* chief priests," "*we* had hoped," "some women of *our* group astounded *us*," "they came back and told *us*," "some of those who were with *us*."

Thereupon, they are reproached by "the only stranger in Jerusalem" who did not understand things as they had understood them. Failing to make their own the hope that stirred in the imagination of the great prophets, the disciples had been imagining a prophet "mighty in deed and in word before God and all the people" (v. 19), gloriously triumphing over the pagan forces of occupation. In their own words, they admit: "We had hoped that he was the one to redeem Israel" (v. 21). Their imagination, proving too limited and closed, had excluded the possibility of a more wonderful entry of God into their history in the person of Jesus, the Christ:

> "Oh, how foolish you are, and how slow of heart to believe all that the prophets had declared! Was it not necessary that the Messiah should suffer these things and then enter into his glory?" (v. 25).

Although these disillusioned disciples had lacked a sense of how the prophets had understood God's way of acting, Jesus himself now draws them into his own way of imagining himself and his mission in the light of Israel's sacred inheritance: "Then beginning with Moses and all the prophets, he interpreted to them things about himself in all the scriptures" (v. 27). The former limitations of the "we" and "our" and "us" are now met with another explanation, as Jesus takes the initiative in breaking the boundaries that grief and failure had imposed. He would always find a way to them, even if they had lost their way to him.

Imagination Transformed

As the disciples approach their destination, Jesus "walked ahead as if he were going on" (v. 28). He had taken the initiative in seeking them out and in addressing them in their fear and defeat. Now, in response, the disciples had to show their own initiative in the light of what had happened as that eventful day was coming to a close. And they do, in fact, respond with a gesture of generous hospitality: "They urged him strongly, saying, 'Stay with us, because it is almost evening and the day is now nearly over'" (v. 29). Jesus accepts and goes in with them and joins them around the table. The path he had traveled with them and the words he now addresses to them are summed up in what has been the experience of the Church down the ages: "He took bread, blessed and broke it, and gave it to them" (v. 30).

The awareness that had been growing within the two disciples now blossomed into a full recognition of their fellow traveler: "Then their eyes were opened, and they recognized him; and he vanished from their sight" (v. 31). Their fellow traveler, Jesus, was no longer a mere stranger meeting them in their fear and explaining what the prophets had predicted long before. Rather, although he vanishes from their sight, he will be forever with them in "the breaking of the bread." This is what he had foretold, that he would not eat and drink with them until the Passover was fulfilled in the Kingdom of God (see Luke 22:14–19). But now, on this day, that kingdom of love and mercy is revealed, and he is present to his disciples, communicating to them all that the kingdom of love and mercy promised.

The disciples' journey which was apparently taking them away from contact with Christ was, in fact, leading them back. Through the cross and resurrection of Jesus, all the signposts of life are rearranged. The two disciples, previously lost and dazed and discussing among themselves "all these things that had happened" (Luke 24:14), now turn to each other in a new energy and joy. As they recall what had been happening, they ask, "Were not our hearts burning within us while he was talking to us on the road, while he was opening the scriptures to us?" (v. 32). The story they originally heard from the women earlier that day had seemed too good to be true—life simply was not like that. Rather, the world of violence, betrayal, and disappointment was the real world. But now they found that what the prophets had promised, what Jesus had taught and predicted, what the women had reported, what the risen Jesus had explained to them and, above all, what God had wrought in Jesus—all proved itself so good that it had to be true.

Carried along with this new conviction, the two disciples hurry back in the final hour of that day of wonders to the city they had intended to leave behind. There they rejoin the apostles and the disciples to find them, like themselves, exulting in the truth: "The Lord has risen indeed!" (v. 34). The two disciples tell their story of "what had happened on the road, and how he had been made known to them in the breaking of the bread" (v. 35).

A time would come, of course, when these two disciples would again leave the city, but this time they would leave as witnesses to the mercy that had been shown to them: "Repentance and for-giveness of sins is to be proclaimed in his name to all the nations, beginning from Jerusalem" (v. 47). On that day, they would travel with the power of the Spirit (see v. 49), pausing only to be re-freshed and nourished by the one who had made himself known to them in the breaking of the bread. Jesus' way of imagining God and the world had possessed them.

∽ 4 ∾
"THE BREAD OF GOD"
(John 6)

The sixth chapter of John's Gospel lies at the heart of what I have been calling the "eucharistic imagination." For that reason, it deserves more extensive treatment.

Images of Abundance (John 6:1–21)

This scene opens on a familiar world of human need and hope: a large crowd has followed Jesus to the other side of the Lake of Galilee "because they saw the signs that he was doing for the sick" (v. 2). Like the new Moses, Jesus has gone up the mountain and sat down there with his disciples. It is near the Feast of Passover, an occasion that always brims with significance for Jews everywhere as they recall the great things God has done for his people. The Gospel suggests that the same God is still at work, about to bring forth something even more wonderful. When Jesus sees the large crowd coming to him, he puts a question to Philip: "Where are we to buy bread for these people to eat?" (v. 5).

There is a special irony in Jesus' question, as it heralds back to Moses, his father in faith. Moses, feeling the burden of responsibility for the people he had led out into the desert, complained to the Lord:

> "Where am I to get meat to give to all this people? For they come weeping to me and say, 'Give us meat to eat!' I am not able to carry all this people alone, for they are too heavy for me. If this is the way you are going to treat me, put me to death at once'" (Numbers 11:13).

But, in this time of fulfillment, Jesus, the new Moses, knows no such frustration. He is not about to drive away anyone the Father has given him (see v. 37). Rather, in that green springtime (see v. 10), he instructs his disciples to make the people recline on the grass, thus evoking the "green pastures" to which the Lord shepherds his flock (see Psalm 23:1–3). Resting there, the people are about to share in an economy that infinitely surpasses the scope of human resources. Neither Philip's estimate of an impossible "two hundred denarii" (v. 7) nor Andrew's remark on the pitiful amount of provisions actually available—"five barley loaves and two fish"(v. 9)—set any limits on the bounty of God: "Jesus took the loaves, and when he had given thanks, he distributed them...; so also the fish, as much as they wanted" (v. 11). After the crowd is satisfied, he instructs the disciples to gather up what is left over, "so that nothing may be lost" (v. 12).

The food for which Jesus had given thanks (see vv. 11 and 33) and the twelve baskets that remain suggest the inexhaustible nourishment that the Church will receive from the Eucharist in the ages ahead.

The popular response, or course, is ecstatic: "This is indeed the prophet who is to come into the world" (v. 14). But Jesus does not feed off the impulsive movement of the crowd; rather, the Father's will is his food (see John 4:34) and God has greater gifts in store for him: "When Jesus realized that they were about to come and take him by force to make him king, he withdrew again to the mountain by himself" (John 6:15).

The fall of evening that day (see v. 16) brings with it a deeper experience of the mystery of God at work. Jesus, having removed himself from the bemused crowds, has separated himself from the disciples in a time of darkness and danger. In the most graphic sense, the disciples in the boat are "all at sea," making heavy weather of the lake-crossing against the strong wind (see v. 18), and setting the scene for Jesus to rejoin them. And, indeed, he comes—in the full force of his identity: "It is I; do not be afraid" (v. 20). He who will give himself in the Eucharist dispels their fear. He who is the Word through whom all things have come into being (see John 1:3, 10) brings peace to the world, just as wind blowing where it will (see John 3:8) is a figure of the Spirit leading to a revelation of God's limitless gift. And as the disciples' boat reaches land (v. 21), the saving power of God brings them to a safe place: "He made the storm be still, / and the waves of the sea were hushed. / Then they were glad because they had quiet, / and he brought them to their desired haven" (Psalm 107:29–30). In the often threatened life of the Church, the Eucharist will be a site of renewed strength and hope.

The Next Day of Greater Gifts (John 6:22–40)

The next day dawns (see v. 22) on a crowd of perplexed people. Having lost contact with both Jesus and the disciples, the people cross the sea in search of this Jesus, the giver of the miraculous bread. Sadly, however, they have yet to appreciate that such bread was meant as a sign of a much greater gift:

> When they had found him on the other side of the sea, they said to him, "Rabbi, when did you come here?" Jesus answered them, "Very truly, I tell you, you are looking for me, not because you saw signs, but because you ate your fill of the loaves. Do not work for the food that perishes, but for the food that endures for eternal life, which the Son of Man will give you. For it is on him that God the Father has set his seal" (vv. 25–27).

The crowd's seeming success in finding Jesus in fact reveals that they still have a long way to go. This is evident in the distracted nature of the question concerning the time of Jesus' arrival, and his response emphasizes the demanding reality of the search in which they are involved. Intent on the wondrous physical nourishment they had experienced, the crowd must come to see it as a sign of something more; they must be nourished by another kind of bread. They must come to understand that Jesus has food to offer that is unknown, for his food is found in total surrender to the work of the one who sent him (see John 4:32–34). The food that sustains him and the food that he promises are made of the same ingredients: the energies of eternal life.

Jesus is the source of eternal life because the Father has irrevocably set his seal upon him, legitimating his mission and underwriting the gift he offers: "the bread *of God*" (John 6:33, emphasis added). The promised reality of the Eucharist bears the signature of the Father—just as it will come to be countersigned by the lives of countless future believers.

When Jesus promises this extraordinary gift, the crowd is stirred to a fresh sense of obligation; after all, they are not accustomed to receiving anything for free. They have not yet understood that it is not what *they* have to do, but what *God* is doing and giving that is the crucial issue: "What must we do to perform the works of God?" (v. 28). Jesus replies, "This is the work of God, that you believe in him whom he has sent" (v. 29). Still, however, the people are trapped in a world of human calculations, and Jesus and his gift must be made to fit into the dimensions of their familiar world:

> So they said to him, "What sign are you going to give us then, so that we may see it and believe you? What work are you performing? Our ancestors ate the manna in the wilderness; as it is written, 'He gave them bread from heaven to eat.'" Then Jesus said to them, "Very truly, I tell you, it was not Moses who gave you the bread from heaven, but it is my Father who gives you the true bread from heaven. For the bread of God is that which comes down from heaven and gives life to the world." They said to him, "Sir, give us this bread always" (vv. 30–34).

At least the people are beginning to realize that the crucial issue turns on faith in the true God: the miraculous gift of bread is meant as a sign of something more. In the Mosaic tradition, the gift of heavenly bread had been a precious sign of the nourishing power of the Law. It looked back to the Passover experience of God leading his people and, indeed, bringing them to this critical point. The ancestors ate manna in the desert, for the God of Moses had acted on their behalf. Thus, the marvelous gift of manna symbolized the unfailing, life-giving bread of the Law. Is the bread that Jesus promises a continuance of this—or is he promising something more? If he is promising more, how are the people to know his promise is genuine?

Jesus gives an emphatic reply to their challenge. He first recalls the people to a sense of the ultimate source of what he is promising. God, not Moses, has been the constant principal actor. For even Moses had to pray; and God had acted in answer to his prayer. Jesus assures the people that this God will continue to nourish his people; but now, "it is my Father who gives you the true bread from heaven" (v. 32b). Thus, the Father, anticipating this time of fulfillment, gives the *true* bread, in contrast to all previous forms of nourishment. "The Bread of God" is a gift meant not only for Israel, but for the wider world, in the present and for the future: "For the bread of God is that which comes down from heaven and gives life to *the world*" (v. 33, emphasis added). The divine bounty knows none of the limits of the past.

But the response of the people is still tentative: "Sir, give us this bread always" (v. 34). Their mode of address, although respectful, is not yet that of faith, because their concern is with themselves—"us"—not with the larger world of God's love. They certainly are happy to have a continuous supply of bread that will meet their human needs—provided it leaves their lives undisturbed. It is at this point, then, that Jesus identifies "the bread of God" with himself:

> "I am the bread of life. Whoever comes to me will never be hungry, and whoever believes in me will never be thirsty. But I said to you that you have seen me and yet you do not believe. Everything that the Father gives me will come to me, and anyone who comes to me I will not drive away; for I have come down from heaven, not to do my own will, but the will of him who sent me. And this is the will of him who sent me, that I lose nothing of all that he has given me, but raise it up on the last day. This is indeed the will of my Father, that all who see the Son and believe in him may have eternal life; and I will raise them up on the last day" (vv. 35–40).

Jesus is, in person, the once-and-for-all, never-failing bread of life. The closed world of "us" will be broken open to include all comers, "anyone who believes" (v. 35b). No longer is Israel the exclusive beneficiary of the bread from heaven. Rather, it will be offered to the world of "anyone." Furthermore, the continuing hunger and thirst characteristic of the sages of Israel will now find its satisfaction. In the past, "those who eat me will hunger for more, and those who drink me will thirst for more" (Sirach 24:21, cf. Isaiah 49:10). Now, through the eucharistic gift, that "more" will be made available in him, the bread of life for all. This final gift, however, resides in an as yet undeclared future. But is it being deferred to "the last day" in terms of common conceptions of religious expectation? If not, how much longer will the present hungering and thirsting have to be borne? While something utterly new is being promised now, when will that promise be kept?

If the future is elusive, the tug of the past is clear and strong: "You have seen me, and yet do not believe" (John 6:36). Jesus finds that his hearers are responding from within an horizon bounded by their human preconceptions and calculations. In clinging to the past and interpreting signs of eternal life merely as worldly marvels, potential believers are held back from a complete appreciation of the gift of God (see v. 36). And yet, there is another influence at work. God is acting. The original gift of the Father, extended to all without exception, is the ultimately critical factor (see v. 37a). Those coming to Jesus are part of the "all things" given him by the Father (see John 3:35), to be the recipients of God's gift to the world (see John 3:16; 4:10): God gives his only Son to the world, and gives the world—"all things"—to the Son. Because of this original and continuing giving of the Father, believers will come to the Son (see John 6:37a). Despite the constrictions imposed by the rejection and conflict he faces, Jesus is unreservedly at one with the Father's will. Anyone who comes to him, he "will never drive away" (v. 37b). In that world of many exclusions and rejections, in which even Jesus himself is not accepted by his own (see John 1:11) and in which his followers suffer excommunication from the synagogue (see John 9:34; 16:2), he will not shut anyone out.

The universal love of the Father remains the rule and motive of Jesus' life. A new communion of life with the Father and the Son is in the making (see John 17:21–24). In his coming "down from heaven" (John 6:38)—in that deepest descent into the world of flesh, suffering, and death—a new order of love, healing, and life is unfolding. In him, at this Passover time, past promises are being kept. Jesus will lose nothing of all that the Father has given him. The Father gives and the Father sends—and the Son, given and sent, acts in accord with the conditions of such a gift and such a mission, "that I should lose nothing of all that he has given me" (v. 39a).

The life-giving power of the bread from heaven reaches even into death, and out to all history, even as the generations come and go. Through the ages, the Father continues to love the world (see John 3:16), and Jesus continues to keep all that he has been given to "raise it up on the last day" (John 6:39b). Taking place in him—then and now—is life as the light of all humankind (see John 1:3b–4), and his quickening influence outlasts death and all imaginable worldly endings. The vital factor in human existence is the Father's all-inclusive, life-giving will. The gifts and limitations of the past are superseded, as Jesus promises life to *all*, both *now* and *forever* (John 6:40).

The Source of Life (John 6:41–51)

Then the Jews begin to complain about Jesus because he said, "I am the bread that came down from heaven" (v. 41). They know Jesus, and they wonder, "Is not this Jesus, the son of Joseph, whose father and mother we know? How can he now say, 'I have come down from heaven?'" (v 42).

In the Passover setting of this new gift from heaven, the murmuring of the present generation recalls their ancestors' complaints against Moses. The Israelites of the past, even in their hour of liberation, resisted the promised exodus, dreading the loss of former securities (see Exodus 15:24; 16:2, 7; 17:3). In this Passover, the one Jesus is about to celebrate, that resistance continues. How could this man be the bread from heaven and replace the traditional sources of religious sustenance? Their narrow "we know"— at least what they think they know—is closing them against the possibility of the new gift in their midst. Just as such an attitude enclosed Nicodemus (see John 3:2) in an earthly interpretation of Jesus, so now this later claim to "know" disallows the possibility of Jesus' divine origin. In reply, Jesus concedes, in effect, that his claims are not self-evident; rather, they can be decided only in terms of the One who has sent him:

"Do not complain among yourselves. No one can come to me unless drawn by the Father who sent me; and I will raise that person up on the last day. It is written in the prophets, 'And they shall all be taught by God.' Everyone who has heard and learned from the Father comes to me. Not that anyone has seen the Father except the one who is from God; he has seen the Father. Very truly, I tell you, whoever believes has eternal life. I am the bread of life" (John 6:43–48).

In a piercing reference to the words of Moses—"Your complaining is not against us but against the LORD" (Exodus 16:8)—Jesus declares that it is the Father who sent him who is attracting all to him. It is the Father who acts by that "drawing" which finally will be realized when Jesus himself is lifted up to draw all to himself (see John 12:32). The divine attraction will be complete when the Son raises up on the last day those whom the Father has drawn to him. A new Passover and a new Exodus are taking place. By confining themselves to an earthly identification of Jesus as the son of Joseph, however, these Jews render themselves incapable of recognizing his divine origin and the divine source of the life he offers. They do not see that everything the Son says and does originates in the limitless vitality of God. While God taught Israel through the Law, now all who are truly docile to divine instruction—those whom the Father has sought out as true worshipers in spirit and truth (see John 4:23)—will come to him. Although "salvation is from the Jews" (see John 4:22b), it was never intended to be limited to them. Israel's own faith in the one God of all creation, therefore, is being disconcertingly realized.

Jesus, then, is the center of a new open circle of life in God. As God's Son, he is the Word of an invitation open to all, irrespective of their relation to the Mosaic tradition. If the light of God is to be communicated, it must be received in its full radiance. Jesus gives what he has received; he reveals what he knows. Yet, by conceding, "Not that anyone has seen the Father" (John 6:46a), he acknowledges a problem. Despite the nourishing truths of past revelation, God, in fact, has remained invisible, even to his chosen ones. Now, however, there is a unique exception: a unique divine "visibility" has occurred—in Jesus himself: "He has seen the Father" (v. 46b). The problem of being taught by the God whom no one has seen has reached an unforeseen solution. The Son is God seen and seeable because of his unique relationship to God both "in the beginning" (John 1:1) and in his life in the flesh (see John 1:18). In contrast to the exalted position of Moses in the gift of the Law (John 1:17), Jesus is "full of grace and truth" (John 1:14). The experience of being taught by God is intrinsically connected to believing in the one who has seen God as the condition essential for the possession life eternal: "Whoever believes has eternal life" (John 6:47).

Contrasting the spheres of death and life, Jesus declares that the bread he gives—and is—is truly life-giving: "I am the bread of life" (John 6:48). The former "bread from heaven" was not finally life-giving because of the known fate of the ancestors of this present generation—who "ate the manna in the wilderness" and died (v. 49). Even the greatest figures of the past were enclosed in the domain of death, ruled by a mortality that left God unseen and the promises of God unfulfilled. Now, however, there is a new order of life, unrestricted by death and opened to believers by the one who has seen God: "This is the bread that comes down from heaven, so that one may eat of it and not die" (v. 50). Finally, death has been deprived of its lethal power.

Jesus, the source and form of true life, is the truth by which all else is judged, even death itself. Now it is not death but the Word incarnate, the living bread from heaven, that has the last word: "I am the living bread that came down from heaven. Whoever eats of this bread will live forever" (v. 51a,b). Although Jesus himself would be put to death, and future believers would not be spared their own mortal fate, the human meanings of both life and death are thrown into question by Jesus' promise of a life that defies death. Still, he promises the gift of eternal life in a manner so unconditional that death is consigned to the realm of nonreality.

Although the glory of the cross and resurrection is yet to be revealed, the Father's life-giving, all-embracing will has an immediate effect—for the gift of life does not wait on some form of postmortem existence to be realized. Believers are not to imagine that they must go up to heaven to find true life only after death; rather, this life, through the coming of Jesus, is stirring in their midst. Within this world of flesh and death, the gift of life is available "in person": "I am the living bread" (v. 51a). The natural and cultural symbolism of bread as the nourishment of human life has been transformed. The Word-made-flesh brings life that flows from the Father into the world of flesh. Jesus is passionately intent on being and communicating the true bread of life: "And the bread that I will give for the life of the world is my flesh" (v. 51c). The life-giving God gives what is most intimately his own, "his only Son" (John 3:16); and his Son gives what is most intimately his own—"my flesh"—for the life of the world.

An Unsettling Imagination (John 6:52–59)

When the Jews dispute among themselves, saying, "How can this man give us his flesh to eat?" (v. 52), Jesus says to them, "Very truly, I tell you, unless you eat the flesh of the Son of Man and drink his blood, you have no life in you. Those who eat my flesh and drink my blood have eternal life, and I will raise them up on the last day; for my flesh is true food and my blood is true drink" (vv. 52–55)

Traditional religious categories are understandably at a loss before this startling claim: God? Yes! *This man?* Hardly! Spirit? Yes! *Flesh?* No! Jesus' emphatic realism is, in any literal sense, profoundly shocking. But the Word-made-flesh jolts the imagination into a larger horizon. It is the flesh and blood of the Son of Man, in his God-given solidarity with all human beings, that is the crucial reality—not the limited, enclosed individuality of the fleshly existence that is the polar opposite to the divine realm (see John 7:24; 8:15). Only by truly assimilating what Jesus is, in the flesh and blood of his life-giving mission, will the gift of life be given. The vitalizing reality of the flesh of the Son of Man will appear only in his atoning death and in the gifts that flow from it. And although the fullness of the gift is yet to be disclosed, it is already offered in the present. The sheer physicality of this "eating" (no longer *phagein*, but *trogein* as in John 13:18)[1] underscores the earthly reality of the food that is being offered in the flesh-and-blood reality of the Word dwelling among us. Faith does not have to ascend to some ethereal spiritual sphere above the world; rather, it finds the source of life in our midst, in this world of time and space—and conflict. This eucharistic food and drink has to be received by an equally flesh-and-blood community in the rough-edged reality of its own sufferings and conflicts.

The starkly made, universal offer of this food and drink implies a form of life that has already begun, even if it supposes that history will continue toward some definitive moment of completion. Beginning now, the stream of this endless life reaches beyond all temporal endings and deaths—till "the last day." It will transform the meaning of all dying, all deaths and, in this, it contrasts with the bread that perishes, the bread that Israel's ancestors have eaten. All past forms of sustenance for our earthly journey are now fulfilled in this "true bread" and "true drink."

As believers—whoever they are and whoever they will be—eat and drink the life-giving gift that Jesus embodies, they enter into a life of communion with him that is so intense it can be described as a relationship of mutual indwelling. "Those who eat my flesh and drink my blood abide in me, and I in them" (John 6:56). Although the mission of Jesus will take him to death and render him absent from his disciples in terms of worldly appearances, it will also mean for him a new mode of life and presence within the community of his followers. This community of faith, for its part, will be united in a new humanity in a way that transcends the separations and segregations that had formerly divided it. Believers will dwell in him, and he will be the point of God's communication at which all their experience of God, of themselves, and of their world is transformed.

The source of the mutual indwelling between Jesus and his followers, present and future, is the deathless life of the Father. From him comes the life that is now flowing into the world: "Just as the living Father sent me, and I live because of the Father, so whoever eats me will live because of me" (v. 57). As "the living Father," God is not only not limited by death, but will make the self-giving of the Son in death the form and source of deathless life. Although, in the event, Jesus and his disciples die, the Father does not. As the "living" one, he is the source of Jesus' unqualified promise of eternal life. The gospel's apparent dismissal of the obvious reality of death arises out of an experience of the limitless vitality of God as it will be revealed in the Risen One himself. Under the influence of "the living Father," the death of the Son, along with the inevitable deaths of those who dwell in him, are included in the gift of superabundant life (see John 10:10). For the true disciple, the reality of death is transformed; the living Father, the living Son, and the living community of believers—all are united in one communion of life streaming forth from the source of eternal life, the Father himself. In that realm of life, death loses the deadliness that fear, guilt, and worldly glory project onto it. Thus, dying no longer means leaving life behind; rather dying becomes the way into life without end.

A "Life-Crisis" for the Disciples (John 6:60–71)

Jesus' promise provokes a crisis in a world under the thrall of death. Believers must step beyond what they can cling to—in a dreaded letting-go of all routine securities. Faith must leap over the obstacle posed by fear of the new. It must be ready to receive:

> When many of his disciples heard it, they said, "This teaching is difficult; who can accept it?" But Jesus, being aware that his disciples were complaining about it, said to them, "Does this offend you? Then what if you were to see the Son of Man ascending to where he was before? It is the spirit that gives life; the flesh is useless. The words that I have spoken to you are spirit and life. But among you there are some who do not believe" (vv. 60–64).

God's gift revealed in the free self-gift of the Son intrinsically demands a free acceptance on the part of the believer. God's free gift promises no automatic outcome. Although the disciples are privileged witnesses to Jesus' self-revelation during the storm on the sea (see v. 20), they must continue to hear his command, "Do not be afraid." The prodigality of the gift of God has become a scandal to a world built on human expectations and possibilities. As the people say: "This is a hard saying" (see v. 60). Yet Jesus' response reaches into the secret places of hesitation and fear (see v. 61a, cf. also, 16:1). For his listeners, the word of Jesus is not sufficiently "heavenly"; it is deemed incompatible with traditional ideas of how God is revealed and of how salvation must come about. Still, he meets them at their point of stumbling: "Then what if you were to see the Son of Man ascending to where he was before?" (v. 62). The disaffected disciples are looking for an *ascent* to distant heavenly realms along the lines of great revelation figures of the past—Abraham, Moses, Isaiah, and Enoch. What, in fact, is taking place is the *descent* (see John 3:13) from the now opened heaven (see John 1:51). From the realm of God—whom no one has ever seen (see John 1:18; 6:46)—an all-surpassing gift has been given and a final revelation has been made. Through Jesus, life flows into the world from "the living Father" (v. 57). There would, indeed, be an ascent (see John 20:17), but only because a unique descent from above into the reality of this world had been accomplished.

In a sense, the wavering disciples are so caught between heaven and earth as not fully to inhabit either. At one extreme, confined to "the flesh" of their defensive judgments, they are closed to things that are from above. On the other hand, because of a misplaced sense of what is "from above," they are scandalized by the presence of the Word-made-flesh. Admittedly, the world of the flesh cannot, of itself, generate the deathless life that Jesus offers, for "it is the spirit that gives life; the flesh is [of no avail]" (6:63a). Still, the Word has come in the flesh, into the midst of what is earthly, and communicated the things that are from above (see John 3:12): "The words that I have spoken to you are spirit and life" (John 6:63b). The life-giving power of the Spirit operates in the world of the flesh even though there is nothing on the level of the flesh to explain either its origin or its promise. In the free air of God's action, the breath of the Spirit still blows where it wills (see John 3:8). Thus the believer is led slowly to appreciate the overwhelming novelty of the flesh of Jesus as belonging to the Word incarnate. The domain of the flesh, of itself, promises no life without end. True life derives "not of blood or of the will of the flesh or of the will of man, but of God" (John 1:13). But because the Word, turned in the beginning toward God (1:1), became flesh, "what took place in him was life" (1:3b–4). Thus Jesus in the flesh, and in giving his flesh for the life of the world (6:51), reveals the unseeable God within this world (see 1:18) and communicates eternal life within it.

Jesus accepts that, in the world of the flesh in which he speaks and acts, there would be doubt and betrayal: "But among you there are some who not believe" (6:64). For him, however, his

Father's love for the world is the fundamental factor, so that he will not drive away any who come to him (see v. 37), since those who come do so because of the Father's gift (v. 65). Seeing signs and hearing words are not enough. The Father's "seeking" (4:23) and "drawing" (6:44) of believers lead from the signs and anticipations of the divine gift to its reality, actualized in the coming of his only Son, in the words he speaks, and in the bread of life he gives.

Although the saving will of God is all-inclusive, all, whether Jew or Christian, share in the same temptation—the need to make Jesus fit into a familiar world. The unhappy outcome is, therefore, predictable: "Many of his disciples turned back and no longer went about with him" (v. 66). They fall back into their old worlds undisturbed by the Word, no longer moving with him along the way of a new Passover.

As the crowd drifts, Jesus poses a question to the inner circle of the twelve: "Do you also wish to go away?" (v. 67). Only through a continually renewed decision to follow him can the chosen disciples continue to experience the gift that is offered. For them, too, it is still possible to turn back to old securities. But the Father is at work—and his influence is evident in Peter's question: "Lord, to whom can we go? You have the words of eternal life" (v. 68). When heaven has been opened (see John 1:51), there is no other resting place. Peter thus acknowledges that the words of Jesus are, indeed, "spirit and life" (6:63). Still, his confession goes further: "We have come to believe and know that you are the Holy One of God" (v. 69).

In this statement of Peter, the "Rock," the purest motive of faith in Jesus is articulated for the first time in the gospel. Here, the divine origin of Jesus is confessed. He is acknowledged to be the Holy One *of God*—consecrated by God in a special intimacy and mission. True faith in Jesus does not consist in situating him in this world, but in recognizing that he comes from beyond this world—from the realm of the invisible, living God himself.

Peter, while speaking for the twelve, gives expression to the demands made on all believers. Even those who have been especially chosen by Jesus himself must live out the reality of a decision; after all, human freedom remains ambivalent. Indeed, one of the twelve will prove to be "a devil" (v. 70), an agent of the ruler of this world (see John 14:30).

While later theologies will rightly emphasize the "real presence" of the Body and Blood of Jesus in the sacramental symbols of the bread and wine, the gospel takes us first of all into what might be called the "eucharistic imagination" of Jesus that his disciples are invited to share. He who alone has seen the Father (see 6:46) imagines his relationship to his disciples as the sustaining, life-giving bread that bears the full reality of self-giving love for all whom the Father has given him. The Eucharist arises out of the imagination of Jesus intent on communicating the Father's deathless life to the world. His imagination is communicated to those who receive him to form them into a eucharistic way of life and conduct. This point will be driven home when we consider that imaginative act on the part of Jesus—the washing of his disciples feet (see 13:1–17).

By being drawn into his imagination, by dwelling in him as he dwells in them, his followers awaken to a new sense of identity. The horizon of their existence is no longer bounded by death, but moves in a stream of life emanating from "the living Father" himself. The defining factor is the limitless, transforming vitality of God, not the inevitability of death—around which cluster all the feelings of dread, guilt, and separation from God. The eucharistic imagination, therefore, is determined by a life-source flowing out to all, catching believers up into its unfailing stream and bearing them on to deathless fulfillment: "Just as the living Father sent me, and I live because of the Father, so the one who eats me will live because of me....The one who eats this bread will live forever" (6:57–58).

∽ 5 ∼
EUCHARISTIC CONDUCT
(John 13)

I
n chapter 13 of John's Gospel, the eucharistic imagination of Jesus depicted in John 6 is communicated to his disciples to inspire a eucharistic conduct and way of life. In the context of the last meal he shares with them before his death, Jesus gives the supreme example of such conduct by washing his disciples' feet, just as he gives them his "new commandment." Where the other gospels tell of his "institution" of the Eucharist, John's Gospel takes us into its deeper meaning.

The Realm of Love (John 13:1–3)

Now before the feast of the Passover, Jesus knew that his hour had come to depart from this world to the Father. Having loved his own who were in the world, he loved them to the end (v. 1).

In his mission from the Father, Jesus has been present at a number of feasts—the Sabbath, Tabernacles, and previous Passovers. In the "now" of this decisive hour, however, we see that all previous celebrations have led to this crucial Passover in which the life-giving love of the Father will be disclosed. As Jesus moves from this world to the Father, he brings to fulfillment the movement that the Exodus of Israel prefigured. But now it is the world as a whole, represented in his beloved disciples, that is involved. Recall that John the Baptist had previously acclaimed him as the "Lamb of God" (1:29); now, the Passover lamb customarily slaughtered and eaten at the Jewish feast is replaced by what it had prefigured. The Father has given this "Lamb *of God*" into the world, and he will die and be consumed. Through the shedding of his blood, the sin of the world will be taken away and its violence disarmed (see 1:29).

John's Gospel provides ample evidence of the world's self-destructive predicament. Nonetheless, the cleansing blood of this Lamb is the Father's gift. God has loved the world in giving his Son right into its state of alienation (see 3:16; 10:17; 1 John 1:7; 2:2; 4:10). The Son, as the Lamb of *God* and the Good Shepherd, lays down his life for those the Father has given him. By "Fathering" the Son in this extreme of self-giving, the generative love of God counters the perversely productive power of evil and introduces into human existence a new life-form through the gift of eternal life—and the "children of light" are born (see 12:36). Because the Father has acted in lovingly giving into the world what is his most intimate possession, namely, his only Son, the way of a final exodus is opened.

All through Jesus' mission, his imagination had been stretching forward to the "hour" that has now arrived, when "Jesus knew that his hour had come" (13:1b). It is *his* hour, since this was the moment for which he lived in surrender to the Father's will (see 2:4; 4:21, 23; 7:30; 12:23, 27). And in "his hour" the whole course of human history will be condensed and fulfilled. In this hour, the Father is creating a new relationship between himself and the world through the sending of his Son—the Word in whom all things came into being (see 1:3). All time and all creation are gathered into this hour in which the union between the Father and the Son will be revealed—and this union is the master-key to the meaning of the gospel. Since "he was in the beginning with God" (1:2), the union implied in that original beginning overflows to be the field of a new unity among the scattered children of God (see 11:52).

As he turns to the Father in this hour, Jesus expresses the fundamental dynamic of his existence: "to depart from this world and go to the Father" (13:1b). In life, and now in the death he is about to die, Jesus is moving toward the Father. While the Word was turned to him in the beginning (John 1:1), the otherwise "unseen God" is now to be made known. The only Son will reveal the Father by virtue of the heart-to-heart relationship he enjoys with the one from whom he came (see 1:18b). Jesus has passed through a world of conflicts, divisions, rejection, and terminal antagonism—

both in regard to the true God and to himself. Yet he has never been deflected from his intention to open that world to the Father's life-giving presence. Now the human history of the Word-become-flesh is coming to its fulfillment. But his departure will make him present in another way—in a communion of life and love that his disciples will share with him.

Jesus' movement toward the Father brings the most intense manifestation of his love for his own: "Having loved his own who were in the world, he loved them to the end" (13:1c). By going to the God who so loved the world, he embodies the limitless extent of the Father's love. His self-surrender to the Father, in fact, mean his self-giving for the life of the world. His disciples, described here as "his own," are set in contrast to the representatives of the world who excluded the Word by which it was created, enlivened, and enlightened (see 1:3–4, 10, 11). Yet, through those who have received him, the world is now opened to the glory of the life-giving love at work. Jesus' love for the Father and for the world goes beyond all limits, and the excess of this love will be enacted in the cross itself, "the end" which marks the unreserved measure of God's gift (see 3:34). Ultimately, out of this excess of love, the eucharistic life of the Church is formed, and finds a language in which to express its deepest meaning.

The eucharistic features of this final supper are intensified as Jesus washes the disciples feet—despite the power of evil at work: "The devil had already put it into the heart of Judas son of Simon Iscariot to betray him" (13:2). Love gives itself, not only in the teeth of the murderous designs of the ruler of this world, but even despite the disciple's betrayal. Love goes "to the end," even where a murderous force is intent on achieving its own ends by organiz-ing the world to do away with its Savior. Yet Jesus is totally be-holden to the utter bounty of God's love: "Jesus, knowing that the Father had given all things into his hands, and that he had come from God and was going to God…" (v. 3). Whatever the power of evil, everything is subjected to his Father's design. All things had been given him as the Father's gift. Nothing, and no one, is left in the hands of others—even as they pursue their antagonistic course leading to Jesus' betrayal and execution. The Father is giving his only Son to the world in order to open it, even at its darkest point, to the radiance of true life. The whole world is implicated. The

Father has given *all things* into his hands. Nothing is left outside of God's love for the world (see 3:16).

The "Example" of Love (John 13:4–17)

Jesus' gesture of washing the disciples' feet occurs in a context saturated with the significance of the Father's love—for both Jesus himself and for all the Father has given him. By taking off "his outer robe..." (v. 4), Jesus is acting in accord with the Father's will and modeling his action on what the Father has done. Through this humble action, he undermines the glory of this world, thereby giving expression to the only truth that can counter the deceit of the devil's designs. Jesus had come to Jerusalem seated on an ass (see 12:14) and had identified himself as the Good Shepherd who lays down his life for his sheep. He had spoken of the grain of wheat falling into the ground and of the glory of God to be revealed through his being lifted up on the cross. In washing his disciples' feet, he symbolically recapitulates his previous words and deeds. Moreover, he anticipates the full meaning of the hour that has now arrived, and so discloses the deepest meaning of the Eucharist in the life of the Church.

Still a prey to the expectations and standards of the glory of this world, however, Peter protests (see 13:6–8). But Jesus replies that what he is now doing for his disciples implies something essential in their relationship to him. They are summoned to be one with him in his relationship to the Father and in his God-given mission: "Unless I wash you, you have no share with me" (v. 8b). In response, Peter gives extravagant consent to what is being asked (see v. 9), even though he does not realize its implications (see vv. 36–38). Still, the point is made: no disciple can witness to the truth save by experiencing the extreme of Jesus' love for "his own."

Nonetheless, it is a matter of freedom; and freedom means the capacity to refuse. In recording Jesus' reading of Judas's intentions at this point (see vv. 10–11), the gospel expresses the determination of love to be true to itself even in the face of those who hide from it. In other words, the divine momentum of this hour must be sought on a plane above the machinations of the world's evil. To the degree that the eucharistic community enters into the real meaning of Jesus' gesture, they are conformed to the self-giving existence of the one they have accepted as "Teacher and Lord" (vv. 12–14). Communion with him means conformity to his self-giving love: "You also ought to wash one another's feet" (v. 14). As a consequence, the Christian community can never understand itself as a collection of isolated and defensive individuals. Nor for the Christian community is it a matter of simply following the golden rule of loving one's neighbor as oneself. For the followers of Christ must act as Christ acted if they are to become agents of love and unity. To know the God whom Jesus reveals is to be drawn out of ourselves into the conduct of self-forgetful love for others. Just as the grain of wheat must fall to the ground if it is not to remain alone, so too, the disciples of Jesus will follow him on his way to the Father by going out to others in the world of God's love. Those who hate their life in this world keep it for eternal life (see 12:23–25). In entering the movement of Jesus' love, his disciples are transformed. In a later letter of John we read: "We know love by this, that he laid down his life for us— and we ought lay down our lives for one another" (1 John 3:16). To follow Jesus is to be involved in the practice of love: "Let us love, not in word or speech, but in truth and action" (1 John 3:18). Jesus' disconcerting gesture of washing the disciples' feet will forever unsettle the celebration of the Eucharist with the question, "How does God's love abide in anyone who has the world's goods and sees a brother or sister in need and yet refuses help?" (1 John 3:17). The form of lasting life will be self-giving love for others:

> "For I have set you an example, that you also should do as I have done to you. [Amen, amen, I say to you,] servants are not greater than their master, nor are [the ones sent] greater than the one who sent them" (John 13:15–16).

The "example" Jesus has given is the example *par excellence*. It anticipates his self-giving—right to the limit of death. Jesus gives himself in this way because that is what God is like:

> "The Son can do nothing on his own, but only what he sees the Father doing; for whatever the Father does, the Son does likewise. The Father loves the Son and shows him all that he himself is doing" (John 5:19–20).

As one with the Father, he is the living bread giving himself, in the flesh of his earthly existence, for the life of the world (see John 6:51). Indeed, he is loved by the Father in that he lays down his life in order to take it up again for the life of all, in accordance with the Father's will (see John 10:17–18). The "works" he performed are intended to reveal the communion of life and love existing between himself and the Father (see John 10:38). In this climactic instance of Jesus' love for his disciples, there is to be found the original exemplar, the self-giving love of the Father himself.

For the disciples, of course, there is a consequence. Just as the Son's action derives from the life-giving love of the Father, the disciples must allow themselves to be drawn into such a communion of love and service, "that you also should do as I have done to you" (John 13:15). There is no position in which disciples can locate themselves outside this movement of self-giving love. In his consciousness of being from and for the Father, and at the extreme limit of his love for his own, Jesus declares, "[Amen, amen, I say to you,] servants are not greater than their master, nor are [the ones sent] greater than the one who sent them" (v. 16). The mission of the disciples to the world flows from the self-giving reality of God's own love. To know the truth of God in this way means a special kind of conduct: "If you know these things, [blessed are you] if you do them" (v. 17). In the context of considerable disunity and scandal, one early community of disciples was recalled to the heart of the gospel with these words: "Beloved, let us love one another, because love is from God; everyone who loves is born of God and knows God" (1 John 4:7). As the ancient hymn from the Liturgy of Holy Thursday sings, *"Ubi caritas et amor, Deus ibi est"* ("Where there is charity and love, that is where God is").

Light in Darkness (John 13:18–32)

The new commandment inspires an outgoing, expanding movement of love and service. But the "problem of evil" must be faced, meaning that love must face rejection and betrayal. It is not about to be defeated by contradiction; rather, it will manifest itself more fully. Although Jesus both chooses (see v. 18) and sends (see v. 20) his disciples, there will be resistance: "The one who ate my bread has lifted his heel against me" (v. 18). Biblical scholars note here that the gospel, in citing Psalm 41:9, uses the very physical word to "eat" (*trogein*) that it previously used in a strong eucharistic sense in Jesus' statement, "Unless you *eat* the flesh of the Son of Man" (John 6:53, emphasis added). The point is clear: although, in defiance of all human logic, the bread of life has been offered to all, even those specially chosen by Jesus will know fragility and confusion. Even Peter will deny him (see John 13:38). Jesus reminds his disciples that it is the all-embracing love of the Father that determines the unfolding of events. God himself will be revealed in his proper glory not only despite but even because of the betrayal the Son will suffer: "When it does occur, you may believe that I am he" (v. 19). The life-giving presence of God, acting beyond any human calculation or limits, is involved.

But God acts through the welcome and hospitality characteristic of the Church's eucharistic community: "Very truly, I tell you, whoever receives one whom I send receives me; and whoever receives me receives him who sent me" (v. 20). As the Father sends the Son, Jesus sends his disciples—and whoever receives the disciple, receives the Son and the one who sent him (see v. 20b). In this way, the chasm between what is above and what is below is overcome, and Jesus' mission finds its completion in our welcoming. In this exercise of hospitality, the movement of God's love reaches into the world. The mission "from above" must be met with a welcoming "from below," as future believers receive the disciples and, through them, receive both Jesus and the Father. Through this welcoming response the scattered children of God are gathered into one (see 12:52).

This "oneness," however, does not mean a merging of identities. In the new communion of life that is in the making, the Father, the Son he has sent, and those sent by Jesus are received in their respective identities. Understand that in the realm of love, different identities are not abolished, but affirmed in the hospitality that marks the reality of true communion built on mutual relationships. The Father's house of "many dwelling places" has room for all (see 14:2). Later, Jesus will pray "that they may all be one. As you, Father, are in me, and I am in you, may they also be in us....[May they] be one, as we are one, I in them and you in me, that they may be completely one" (17:20–23).

Yet the waves of communion emanating from the Father break on the jagged rock of resistance; a diabolic design is also at work (see 13:27). The light will shine, but only in contrast to the deepest darkness (see v. 30b). The self-gift of Jesus will be accomplished in the context of intimate betrayal. At the onset of the passion, when he is distressed in spirit and so aware of the fragility of his disciples, he predicts that "one of you will betray me" (v. 21b). One of his own will set himself outside the communion that has been built on mutual love and welcome. Instead of "receiving," this disciple will opt for betrayal.

Although the ensuing discussion indicates the limited perspective of the disciples, Jesus' love for his own remains true to itself. It will not be reduced to anything else; rather, it will go to the end. The will of the Father will be accomplished only in the vulnerability of love—so much so that Jesus actually uses a gesture of love to identify his betrayer. At the last meal they share together, Jesus gives Judas a fragment of the eucharistic bread: "It is the one to whom I give this piece of bread" (v. 26). The traitorous disciple, however, rejects the excess of love Jesus has shown him (see v. 1), "the example" his master has given (see v. 15), and the hospitality symbolized in the eucharistic "bread." As a result, the disaffected disciple chooses to be part of the Satanic design at work (see v. 27a). Having opted for betrayal rather than the hospitality of true communion, Judas moves from the circle of light—the communion existing between the Father, the Son, and the disciples. He goes into the outer darkness where the ruler of this world waits to accomplish his design: "So, after receiving the piece of bread, he immediately went out. And it was night" (v. 30). Although this night had fallen, the Son shows an unreserved acceptance of the will of the Father as it works even in that outer world of violence and death. Jesus actually frees Judas to act his part: "Do quickly what you are going to do" (v. 27b). Yet the Father is at work: in the glory to be revealed, even this darkness is not dark:

> If I say, "Surely the darkness shall cover me,
>   and the light around me become [dark],"
> even the darkness is not dark to you;
>   the night is as bright as the day,
>   for darkness is as light to you (Psalm 139:11–12).

Thus Judas's nocturnal exit comes to mean, in the logic of the gospel, that the light of glory—of a love that refuses to be anything but itself—begins to shine: "When he had gone out, Jesus said, 'Now the Son of Man has been glorified, and God has been glorified in him'" (v. 31). As events move toward the lifting up of the Son on the cross (see John 1:51; 3:14; 6:27, 53; 8:28; 12:23), he will be glorified as God's revelation. The divine glory, subverting the glory of this world and its ruler, will shine forth (see John 1:14; 2:11; 5:44; 7:18; 11:4, 40; 12:41, 43). The Father and the Son, united in love, will glorify one another: "If God has been glorified in him, God will also glorify him in himself and will glorify him at once" (John 13:32). Here we see clearly that the mutual love called for in the example of the foot-washing (see v. 15) has its radical explanation in the loving relationship existing between the Father and the Son. In this it contrasts with the Satanic glory of this world, which can accomplish its purpose only through deceit, disunity, and murder.

The Way of Love (John 13:33–38)

Still, the hour of glory will mean Jesus' departure, when he is violently removed from the scene. And although both the Jews (see 7:34) and the disciples (see v. 33) will experience his absence, neither party will understand the Father-ward direction of Jesus' path. Only the Son can enter into the realm of the Father, for his glory is outside all human capacity and expectation: "Where I am going, you cannot come" (v. 33). And yet the realities of his departure and the subsequent absence experienced by the "little children" he leaves behind (see v. 33a) lead him to disclose the way in which his disciples can follow him into realm of the Father. Because he has chosen the disciples for his own (see v. 18), they have not allied themselves with "the children of the devil" (see 8:39–47). Jesus has given them the gift of his "example" (13:15). Now he makes them another gift:

> "I give you a new commandment, that you love one another. Just as I have loved you, you should love one another. By this everyone will know that you are my disciples" (13:34–35).

Jesus' departure to the Father creates a space in the world for a new community of love. In the midst of the world's darkness, a luminous clearing will be brought about, opened up by Jesus' unreserved love for his own. Thus, everything he has done and taught has its origins in the Father (see 7:16; 8:26,29,38; 12:49–50). If the disciples, then, obey this new commandment, not only will they be following the way of the Son, they will also enter into the movement of the Father's all-embracing love. Even the small scale of their own mutual love will have its place in showing the world the self-giving love that reigns in the realm of the Father. The logic of Jesus' "new commandment" is sharply expressed in the First Letter of John:

> We love because he first loved us. Those who say, "I love God," and hate their brothers or sisters, are liars; for those who do not love a brother or sister whom they have seen, cannot love God whom they have not seen" (4:19–20).

One of the disciples will betray him, and the rest will desert him; Peter himself will deny him. Yet, despite their ignorance and their various refusals to follow him on his path to the Father (see vv. 36–38), the way will nonetheless be opened: "Where I am going, you cannot follow me now; but you will follow" (v. 36b). The love that has gone "to the end" for the disciples (see v. 1) will be the love that enables them to follow their "Lord and Master" on his way to the Father. They will rejoin Jesus in the love that motivated his entire existence. In the light of the glory to be revealed, "they will follow"—and finally recognize that "we have known and believe the love that God has for us" (1 John 4:16).

With the coming of this hour in which God's universal love will be revealed, the meaning of the Eucharist comes into focus. "God" is not an object possessed by connoisseurs of "religious experience." Rather, God is a mystery of self-giving love, and what most characterizes the divine life is love for the other. For Jesus, the Father is the great Other to whom he is turned. But in turning to the Father, the Son is impelled to give himself for all whom God loves, the many others—the disciples and those who will believe through their witness. The way of Jesus "upward" to the Father is, at the same time, necessarily "outward" to the world. He washes the disciples' feet—demonstrating that the supreme moment of love is not an escape from the world but a deeper involvement with it. This remains—and will remain—a disconcerting dimension in Christian life. The Eucharist, even as it praises and glorifies God, demands mutual love and service among those who celebrate it. As they turn with the Son to face the Father, they are inescapably faced with the all-too-familiar other, to be loved and served in accord with Jesus' example and new commandment. To love God means loving others; worshiping the Father entails dedication to all God's children—our brothers and sisters.

The spaciousness of the Father's house (see 14:2), into which Jesus goes to prepare a place for those who follow him, breathes an overwhelming hospitality. As the Son, Jesus originally inhabits that spaciousness—yet to it he now goes to prepare a place for his followers. He lays down the rules of God's household by washing his disciples feet and exhorting them to do likewise. In the realm of the Father, love rules. Even the traitorous disciple has been offered the eucharistic fragment, the symbol of Jesus' complete self-gift.

A eucharistic imagination sees everything changed. God, for example, can no longer be "kept in his place," confined to heaven. Rather, with the coming of Jesus—the Father having sent his son into the world—the world itself loses its self-made boundaries. Heaven is opened (see 1:51). Nor can Jesus be kept in his place, for he is leaving this world for the Father. Even death ceases to be "in place" as an opaque impenetrable limit. Jesus' death will be a "lifting up," the event in which the love of God will be revealed. In the glory of this love, the disciples, too, must move beyond the limits that their selfishness or fear or grief might impose. Jesus' going to the Father draws his disciples with him into a universe of love, and thus no believer can ever live again in self-contained isolation: "Just as I have loved you, you also should love one another" (v. 34). His real presence in the food and drink of the Eucharist demands that it be a true presence in the hearts and conduct of his followers.

⌒ 6 ⌒
THE CONVERTED IMAGINATION

The Eucharist is always celebrated within a life of continuing conversion; we are not instant people. The patience of God—which has time for the whole of our lives—allows us to keep growing toward that final state when the first commandment is fully realized within us: "You shall love the Lord your God with all your heart, and with all your soul, and with all your mind, and with all your strength" (Mark 12:30). Likewise, the second commandment takes its time and unfolds in a growing concern and compassion for our neighbor: "You shall love your neighbor as yourself" (v. 31).

Such a movement of ongoing conversion works on four levels, each being apparent in the manner in which we celebrate the Eucharist. First and most obviously, there is the strictly religious, God-ward dimension: we turn from idols and false gods to the one living God. In a progressively unreserved surrender to the Trinitarian love that has been revealed to us, we adore, thank, and praise the God whose gifts are communicated to us in the Eucharist, and we give ourselves over to the Divine Will. In this respect, each community, by celebrating the Eucharist, hears the Johannine counsel, "Little children, keep yourselves from idols" (1 John 5:21).

The second aspect of conversion involves love of neighbor. There can be no real surrender to God without the moral dimension of love for our neighbor, especially for those with whom we celebrate the Eucharist: "For those who do not love a brother or sister whom they have seen, cannot love God whom they have not seen" (1 John 4:20).

Third, this process of conversion must involve an openness to the truth that God has revealed, and a commitment to explore that truth. The Eucharist educates our minds to seek, beyond all worldly appearances, cultural prejudices, private fantasies, and personal projections—the decisive reality that gives meaning and purpose to our lives. In this sense, we speak of the "real presence" of Christ to us in the flesh-and-blood reality of our human existence: "Every spirit that confesses that Jesus Christ has come in the flesh is from God" (1 John 4:2). This kind of real presence is opposed to any lofty spirituality incapable of imagining that God's love could have such a human outcome. In short, the Eucharist nourishes and challenges us with the truth of the Incarnation.

This does not mean that our imagination is left out or dismissed as useless. After all, we must love God with our whole heart and soul and mind, and that surely includes our imagination. Hence, there is a fourth aspect of conversion—our human imagination—without which our conversion to Christ lacks passion and creativity. By meditating, say, on the traditional Joyful, Sorrowful, and Glorious Mysteries of the rosary, we let the inexpressible mystery of God enter into our imagination, and we begin to experience ourselves as participants in the gospel story. When the truth of God's love affects our imagination, it not only heals our imaginative lives of fearful and distorted images of God—and of ourselves—but also inspires something deeply positive.

We have a remarkable instance of this aspect of conversion when faith inspires great art in music, painting, sculpture, and poetry. Saint Thomas Aquinas, for example, left us not only his profound philosophical and theological reflections on the Eucharist but also the great hymns, *"Adoro Te"* and *"Lauda Sion."* The Scriptures themselves abound in instances of a transformed imagination. One of special beauty is found in the Letter to the Hebrews, as it reflects on the special character of the revelation that has taken place in the New Testament. Although the Eucharist is not mentioned explicitly in this passage, it is hard to imagine that these words could have been written without an intimate experience of the eucharistic liturgy in the daily life of the Church:

You have not come to something that can be touched, a blazing fire, and darkness, and gloom, and a tempest, and the sound of a trumpet, and a voice that made the hearers beg that not another word be spoken to them....But you have come to Mount Zion and to the city of the living God, the heavenly Jerusalem, and to innumerable angels in festal gathering, and to the assembly of the firstborn who are enrolled in heaven, and to God the judge of all, and to the spirits of the righteous made perfect, and to Jesus, the mediator of a new covenant, and to the sprinkled blood that speaks a better word than the blood of Abel (Hebrews 12:18–24).

I am suggesting, then, that the Eucharist shapes and inspires a deeper conversion on different levels—religious, moral, intellectual, and imaginative. If we are to love God with our whole heart and soul and mind and strength, the Eucharist is the form of that "wholeness" into which we must enter. As the "whole heart" of the Church, the Eucharist inspires our hearts to expand to the dimensions of God's love. As the "whole soul" of the community's worship, it gives soul and imagination to the life of faith. As the "whole mind" of that living faith, it brings us into contact with the whole truth of what has been revealed. As the "whole strength" of the Church, it supports us in our weakness and nourishes us with the sustenance we need on our pilgrim way.

The movement of eucharistic conversion affects our imagination, suggesting appropriate images, priorities, and attitudes. I will illustrate this point under five headings dealing with "Sacrifice," "Holy Communion," "Judgment," "Thanksgiving and Praise," and "Love."

Eucharistic Conversion: Sacrifice

The language and symbols of sacrifice are deeply embedded in our biblical and liturgical expression. In New Testament times, the category of "sacrifice" was part of a living language. Especially for Christians of Jewish background there was the whole ritual activity of the Temple to call on, providing a rich symbolic way of speaking of our relationship to God and the difference Christ has made. The rich and subtle argument of the Letter to the

Hebrews seeks to demonstrate how all the sacrificial rituals of the Old Testament have been brought to an unsurpassable fulfillment in the "sacrifice" of Christ: "But when Christ had offered for all time a single sacrifice for sin...he has perfected for all time those who are sanctified" (Hebrews 10:12, 14). Something momentous and all-decisive has been achieved:

> Therefore, my friends, since we have confidence to enter the sanctuary by the blood of Jesus, by the new and living way that he opened for us through the curtain (that is, though his flesh), and since we have a great priest over the house of God, let us approach with a true heart in full assurance of faith, with our hearts sprinkled clean from an evil conscience and our bodies washed with pure water. Let us hold fast to the confession of our hope...for he who has promised is faithful. And let us consider how to provoke one another to love and good deeds (Hebrews 10:19–24).

The first eucharistic prayer calls on God to accept our present offering as a continuation and completion of three sacrificial offerings recorded in the Old Testament—that "of your servant Abel," "the sacrifice of Abraham, our father in faith," and "the bread and wine offered by your priest Melchisedech." This liturgy of the New Testament realized in the Eucharist involves even the angels: "We pray that your angel may take this sacrifice to your altar in heaven." Finally, at the summit of the eucharistic sacrifice, we receive the "sacred body and blood of your Son" in order that we be "filled with every grace and blessing." For early Christians of pagan background—those who did not have the Old Testament traditions as part of their history—there was the experience of temple sacrifices that figured so largely in the religious ritual of the state and even in the more mundane considerations of where to get a comparatively inexpensive meal of meat (as we remarked in chapter two dealing with 1 Corinthians).

All in all, however exotic it may appear today, the rhetoric of sacrifice is deeply embedded in our inherited religious language, even if now we are a long way removed from any familiarity with temple cults. "Sacrifice" is a way of speaking and imagining so elemental that even in our secularized culture it pops up to describe significant forms of self-giving for the sake of others, either in war or in other remarkable instances of dedication and service.

In terms of the eucharistic imagination we have been exploring, a few remarks are in order, while granting that this theme is one of immense complexity.[1] The striking thing is that, however vague and removed from our culture, "sacrifice language" still can be used in a way that makes imaginative sense in describing how God, Christ, and the Church are involved in each eucharistic celebration. It is not so much as though there were some general notion of sacrifice that is somehow applied in a Christian and eucharistic sense—for scholars are in endless dispute on what "sacrifice in general" could possibly mean. Rather, it is more that self-giving of Christ on the cross redeems and brings to fulfillment everything the human heart wanted to express regarding its relationship to God in its ritual vocabulary of sacrifice, offering, priesthood, victim, and temple.

I am not suggesting that the meaning of such a richly symbolic ritual can be reduced to clear statements. Still, the language of sacrifice seems to work on the level of heart and imagination with a special meaningfulness and evocative power. Although our everyday pragmatic culture may have long forgotten any historical association with ancient temples and rituals, somehow the human heart has not. Whenever the heart attempts to express the excess of love, for example, it speaks the language of sacrifice. Consider the following examples, drawn from the third eucharistic prayer.

This first instance shows how complex and rich Christian sacrificial language is. As faith turns to God in the eucharistic celebration, we are drawn out of ourselves and offer to God in thanksgiving "this holy and perfect sacrifice." The basic reality governing this way of praying is the death, Resurrection, Ascension, and promised return of Jesus. Any self-giving on our part is connected with the Father's own "self-sacrifice" in sending his Son for our salvation, and more immediately with the Son's "self-sacrifice" on the cross. Through the presence of the Crucified and Risen One, we can make our own offering—not just of something, but of someone, namely Jesus himself; and not just as though he were apart from us, say, as confined to the past, but as one involving us now in his own self-surrender to God:

Calling to mind the death your Son endured
    for our salvation,
his glorious resurrection and ascension into heaven,
and ready to greet him when he comes again,
we offer you in thanksgiving this holy and living sacrifice.[2]

Thus, in performing this holy and living sacrifice, three elements are implied—of an ascending order of significance. First, "we offer": we are stepping out of selves and going beyond ourselves in an act of surrender to God. Second, we offer "in thanksgiving" (that is, in *Eucharistia*): there is a self-offering that is in response to God's own gift. In this regard we are not intending to call down on ourselves God's favor, as though God's grace was dependent on what we do. Rather, the opposite is the case. We are acting in this "holy," "living," sacrificial manner because God has acted first, thereby enabling the self-surrender we intend to express. And third, all our sacrificial action derives from our communion with Christ as we "call to mind" the various dimensions of the paschal mystery (his death, Resurrection, and Ascension) to "eagerly await" the day of his return—the fulfillment of his saving presence in history.

Within this general way of connecting the whole mystery of Christ with the eucharistic celebration, an important point emerges. The Father is asked to look with favor on the offering of the Church, and to see the self-giving love of Jesus at the heart of it, nourishing us with his body and blood and filling us with his Holy Spirit, so that we will live in union with him and his mission. Thus, the Eucharist is a "holy and living sacrifice," as well as the reconciling presence of Jesus himself as the "victim" by whose self-giving we have been reconciled to the Father:

Look with favor on your Church's offering,
and see the Victim whose death has reconciled us
    to yourself.
Grant that we, who are nourished by his body and blood,
may be filled with his Holy Spirit,
and become one body, one spirit in Christ.[3]

There are two major points to be noted here. First, it is not as though God's mind is somehow changed or appeased by the sufferings of his Son, as if to suggest that Jesus' death brought about a change of heart in God. No, the Father is the main agent: "See the Victim whose death has reconciled us to yourself." Everything that the Son does and suffers derives from the reconciling love of the Father: "All this is from God, who reconciled us to himself through Christ....God was [in Christ] reconciling the world to himself" (2 Corinthians 5:18–19).

The second important point to note is that the Father's reconciling love explains why his Son is a "victim." Jesus, of course, is not victimized by his own Father. But because the Son's mission is to witness to the limitless extent of the Father's love for the world, he is necessarily exposed to all the violent and murderous forces that structure the world against God and make him seemingly defenseless in his way of love and peace.

Jesus embodies a love that keeps on being love even in the face of the world's terminal lovelessness. In this he identifies himself with all the victims of history who have only God to defend or vindicate them. The great sign indicating that this crucified love is not defeated is the Resurrection—and the Holy Spirit is the continuing inexhaustible energy of this love at work in the world. Hence, Christians pray that they will be nourished by the body and blood of Jesus, thus becoming "one body, one spirit in Christ." By being united with the divine "Victim," we will be saved from contributing to the vicious circle of evil and vengeance. We will not live by making more victims in the world of greed and power; rather, by sharing in his victimhood, we share in his peacemaking love and become its agents and witnesses. In this regard, the Eucharist, because it celebrates the sacrifice of Christ, is a great act of protest and nonviolence, a countercultural stance against the self-serving pride that lives only by victimizing others. The symbols of sacrifice that are so much a part of the Eucharist serve to disarm our hearts, thus "decommissioning," in the depths of our imagination, the lethal weapons of violence and greed used for oppression of the weak and the powerless.

By being united with Christ—and nourished by his deepest reality—we expose ourselves to the reconciling love that determines his whole being, allowing it to flow through us and into a world that desperately needs this one essential, all-renewing resource: "Love is patient; love is kind; love is not envious or boastful or arrogant or rude. It does not insist on its own way; it is not irritable or resentful; it does not rejoice in wrongdoing, but rejoices in the truth. It bears all things, believes all things, hopes all things, endures all things. Love never ends" (1 Corinthians 13:4–8). Thus, we pray:

Lord, may this sacrifice,
which has made our peace with you,
advance the peace and salvation of all the world.[4]

The basic point, then, is this: the Eucharist is a "holy and living sacrifice" in that it unites us with the love of the crucified Jesus. It disturbs our natural selfishness and our all-but-instinctive violence with new responsibilities and new hopes, both of which have their cost. Yet animating all this is the summons to enter into the world of Jesus' imagination. For he refused to imagine life—as it is now or is destined to be—in any way except in terms of the prodigal, all-forgiving, and peacemaking love of God. The language and images of sacrifice and victimhood express the burden of such love, but always with a sense of hope and conviction that all initiative has come from God.

When the Eucharist invites faith to express itself in the difficult and often strange language of sacrifice, we become alert to the variety of idolatrous sacrifices on which human cultures are built, the terrible costs that greed, violence, pride, and self-justification demand. Against these forces of destructiveness, Eucharist places the sacrifice of Christ—the power of love to counter and transform our experience of evil—into the love that "never ends" (1 Corinthians 13:8).

Suffering and dying with Christ means yielding ourselves into the wholeness of God's universe. We are individual grains of wheat falling into the ground of God's infinite mystery, not to remain alone but to spring up and bear fruit for a larger harvest (see John 12:24). By becoming part of this "holy and living sacrifice," we die out of ourselves and are born into an immense communion of life. We are drawn out of limited and defensive individuality of this form of life into the ecstasy of truly personal, other-related existence. We die out of ourselves and are born into the sphere of the Spirit in which self-giving love is the ultimate life form. Our existence as individuals is decentered by our participation in the death of Christ, to find ourselves recentered in the Body of Christ and reintegrated into that new creation in order that "God may be all in all" (1 Corinthians 15:28).

The fourth eucharistic prayer expresses the change of heart and imagination that the eucharistic sacrifice is intended to bring about:

> *In fulfillment of your will*
> *he gave himself up to death;*
> *and by rising from the dead,*
> *he destroyed death and restored life.*
> *And that we might live no longer for ourselves*
> *but for him*
> *he sent the Holy Spirit from you, Father,*
> *as his first gift to those who believe,*
> *to complete his work on earth*
> *and bring us the fullness of grace.*[5]

The self-giving of Jesus releases the Holy Spirit, who takes us out of ourselves, unites us to Christ as our true center, and makes us participants in Jesus' mission to sanctify the world.

The prayer goes on to ask the Father to "look upon this sacrifice which you yourself have prepared for your Church," so that those who share this one bread and cup will be gathered together by the Holy Spirit "into the one body of Christ, a living sacrifice of praise." With these words, we ask God to remember all for whom this offering is made (the pope, bishops, priests, deacons, and all servants in the Church) and all "those who take part in this offering." Included are "those here present and all your people, and all who seek you with a sincere heart." This latter phrase reminds us that the great reconciliation that Christ and the Spirit bring about in believers is also being realized beyond the visible confines of the Church. In ways often unnamed and unnoticed, good people—wherever they follow their conscience and live beyond themselves for the sake of others—are traveling along the way of Christ, empowered by his Holy Spirit.

The eucharistic imagination is always inclusive. It understands itself as expressing not only the explicit faith of the Church but also the language of the human heart in its restless search for God. For to be human is to be continually confronted with the demands of self-sacrifice. The eucharistic imagination finds in the self-sacrifice of Christ Jesus the pattern, the nourishment, and the fulfillment of the movement of the human heart itself.

Eucharistic Conversion: Holy Communion

When the eucharistic imagination is taken beyond itself in self-surrender to God as a "holy and living sacrifice," it is necessarily an opening out to others. It recognizes that the Church is a "holy communion." When the imagination of the Church allows itself to be nourished by this sacrament, the outreach of its communion and the inclusive range of its hope keeps on extending. The Eucharist, after all, is always a community celebration. No matter how isolated and impoverished any particular celebration might be, it can never be purely "private." The community celebrating the Eucharist always represents the whole community of the Church and the wider totality of the world itself.

Because the bread of Jesus is his flesh given for the life of the world (see John 6:51), to receive him is to receive the whole of his body—the whole of his Incarnation as it affects the entire world. In receiving the hospitality of the Father's house of many dwelling places (see 14:2), believers celebrate a God-intended belonging with everyone. To be with God is to be in communion with all who are called to the divine life. As celebrated Swedish poet, Tranströmer wrote, "Each man is a half-open door / leading to a room for everyone."[6] This communal imagination has always been the basis for discerning an authentic Christian celebration of this sacrament. A self-enclosed individualism has no place in the time and space and mood of the Eucharist. To cite Paul: "Because there is one bread, we who are many are one body, for we all partake of the one bread" (1 Corinthians 10:17).

So, too, the eucharistic cup is not a "private communion" with Christ, for it is an entry into the new covenant in his blood poured out for "all," the "many" (see Luke 22:30). Because the Eucharist forms believers into the one body of Christ, it unites them in the unity of the Spirit and in a compassionate solidarity transcending all divisions and segregations. In Christ, we become members of one another in his transformed humanity:

> For just as the body is one and has many members, and all the members of the body, though many, are one body, so it is with Christ. For in the one Spirit we were all baptized into one body...and all were made to drink of one Spirit (1 Corinthians 12:12–13).

The intended result is a sense of our existence as a communion, as a communication within the whole universe of grace. It inspires a sense of solidarity with all, especially in their sufferings:

> If one member suffers, all suffer together with it; if one member is honored, all rejoice together with it. Now you are the body of Christ and individually members of it (1 Corinthians 12:26–27).

In this way, holy Communion incorporates us individually and collectively into the unity of love that characterizes God's own life. As the Father and the Son are who they are by indwelling each in the other, so the unity of the Body of Christ is formed: "As you, Father, are in me and I am in you, may they also be in us, so that the world may believe that you have sent me" (John 17:21). This unity has its source in the Trinitarian mystery of God's own life, while it reaches out to include the whole of the resistant and fragmented world, "that the world may believe."

The sense of a great communion extending through and beyond all time and space is strikingly evoked by the words of Teilhard de Chardin:

> When the priest says the words *Hoc est corpus meum* ["This is my Body"], his words fall directly on the bread and directly transform it into the individual reality of Christ. But the great sacramental operation does not cease at that local and momentary event...these different acts are only the diversely central points in which the continuity of a unique act is split up and fixed, in space and time, for our experience. In

fact, from the beginning of the Messianic preparation up till the Parousia, passing through the historic manifestation of Jesus and the phases of growth of his church, a single event has been developing in the world: the Incarnation, realized, in each individual, through the Eucharist.

All the communions of a life-time are one communion.

All communions of all men now living are one communion.

All the communions of all the men, present, past and future are one.[7]

By nourishing us into such a communal imagination, the Eucharist expresses the continuing conversion of the Church to the universal dimensions of salvation in Christ. It impels to that holy Communion in which the unity of the Son with the Father will be realized among all the scattered children of God (see John 11:53).

Eucharistic Conversion: Judgment

In its objectivity, the real presence of Christ in the Eucharist is a confronting truth. It is at once a judgment on us and a summons to conversion. To this degree it is the presence of the saving but piercing "truth that will make you free" (John 8:32), and it inspires a humility in those who receive it. We are forced to admit that, to the degree our lives have been nourished on the "junk food" of false individualism, or on the "fast food" of life that does not know how to wait and hope, the eucharistic food is apt to provoke an allergic reaction. It is too rich for the sickly constitution of human selfishness. As such, it is distasteful to the unhealthy palate and occurs as a judgment on our condition.[8] In this way, the Eucharist contests the forces that compromise the genuine health of human community. Self-absorption, isolation, and the injustice and greed to which they give rise are anti-Eucharist.

Inasmuch as our individual and corporate lives are frozen in an anti-Eucharistic form, the real presence of Christ is experienced more as a *real absence* in our capacity to imagine the world otherwise. Instead of being the sacrament at the summit and source of the life of the Church, the Eucharist is always in danger of being celebrated as an empty ritual, leaving violence and injustice at work to dismember the one Body of Christ. What is taken to be the "real world"—based on self-centered calculation and self-assertion against others—makes the real presence of Christ unreal, given the priorities that, in fact, structure our lives. Thus the Pauline injunction to "examine yourselves, and only then eat of the bread and drink of the cup" (1 Corinthians 11:28) is a continuing call to conversion. We must "discern the body" (see v. 29a), otherwise believers will be found eating and drinking judgment against themselves (see v. 29b).

Thus each celebration of the Eucharist is a moment of truth that explodes the closed circle of inward-looking piety and confronts it with the awkward reality of the cross of Jesus' self-giving love. To this degree, the eucharistic community is never complete. Against the bias that tends to exclude and ignore others as beyond the reach of God's redemptive love, the Eucharist discloses dimensions of belonging that are easily ignored. This is the problem Paul had in mind when he wrote: "There is [neither] Jew or Greek, there is [neither] slave or free, there is [neither] male and female; for all of you are one in Christ Jesus" (Galatians 3:28; cf. also, Colossians 3:11). By bringing a community to a point of crisis, the Eucharist represents the conscience of the Church—and we cannot settle for anything less than the whole of Christ. To celebrate his presence and nourish ourselves with his reality entails a commitment to "re-member" the body of the crucified one by making whole that which has been dismembered through lovelessness and violence. As a moment of truth, it is a moment of conversion—to go beyond the alienations, boundaries, polarities, and classes of the given society in order to become a genuinely open community of love and hope for all.[9]

In the kingdom of mustard seeds, the Eucharist is a movement of life and growth. There, in that kingdom, the gift of Christ's real presence exposes the rough, threatening terrain of his real absence. The eucharistic imagination has to confront the sobering reality of ambiguity, failure, and unfinished business. Then, the Church's eucharistic pause on its pilgrim journey is, indeed, a moment of reorientation. Then, any particular gathering, indeed, can feel the Lord's judgment: "But I have this against you, that you have abandoned the love you had at first" (Revelation 2:4). Then, his presence, indeed, is an insistent summons: "Be earnest, therefore, and repent. Listen! I am standing at the door, knocking; if you hear my voice and open the door, I will come in to you and eat with you, and you with me" (Revelation 3:19–20).

Eucharistic Conversion: Thanksgiving and Praise

The pattern of liturgical responses are long familiar:

> **Celebrant:** *Lift up your hearts.*
> **Response:** *We lift them up to the Lord.*
> **Celebrant:** *Let us give thanks to the Lord our God.*
> **Response:** *It is right to give him thanks and praise.*
> **Celebrant:** *Father, it is our duty and our salvation, always and everywhere to give you thanks through your beloved Son, Jesus Christ.*[10]

In the eucharistic sacrament, the Church celebrates and shares its commonwealth: God's saving gift in Christ. It is the sacrament of *Eucharistia*—the Greek word for "thanksgiving." Where the gift of God so extravagantly appears, our response naturally follows: "always and everywhere to give you thanks." God's gift demands recognition—and such thanksgiving certainly acknowledges the original gift of the Father, who "so loved the world" (John 3:16) as to send the Son and pour out the Spirit. The gifts of grace, in turn, imply the prior fundamental gift of God manifest in the creation of the universe which has culminated through the passing of the ages "in these last days," with the coming of the Son "through whom he also created the worlds" (Hebrews 1:2). But the range of thanksgiving extends further: there is the often overlooked ministry of angels—"countless hosts of angels stand before you to do your will; they look upon your splendor and praise you, night and day."[11] Moreover, through the bountiful gift of God, a great community has already come into being, founded on the witness of patriarchs, prophets, and apostles, and enriched by the various graces of the martyrs, saints, mystics, and teachers—the holy ones, known and unknown—who are living presences in the communion of saints. We give thanks because we live in a world of gifts and in a universe of grace. Praise and thanksgiving, in fact, are the first movement of the Christian heart.

And yet words such as *praise, thanksgiving,* and *blessing* can easily drop out of our spiritual vocabulary. In a culture of depression, feelings of ecstatic gratitude and wonder seem beyond the our heart's repertoire. The spiritual creativity that once gave rise to great psalms and hymns, that insisted that this sacrament of the Lord's presence be called *Eucharistia,* now groans beneath the weight of hopelessness and defeat, leaving praise in danger of being reduced to a dutiful liturgical squeak. It is as though the religious imagination has been sucked into a black hole from which no light escapes. While the rigid logic of calculation has muted the language of praise and gratitude, the impulse to praise seems to belong to a naive past and the time of cold-eyed rationality seems to have arrived. The tough consumer world of cost-benefit analysis looks to some measurable outcome, leaving God to compete with the idols of the age. In this milieu, thanksgiving belongs to an alien economy.

In the therapeutic culture of our times, personal affirmation is recognized as a valued activity. The more uprooted we are from the eucharistic universe, the more delicate and vulnerable we seem to have become. Unless we are surrounded by a circle of affirmation, our worth is undermined, and we become dependent on the admiration of others. To this degree, praise has become synonymous with care for the fragile and the needy, a demand for psychological well-being. There is a good point here: we are social beings, but the supposedly self-made individual is living in an illusory world. In the absence of any cosmic affirmation of our worth, the helping professions try to fill the gap as best they can. It can be, then, that to talk of praising and thanking God appears as a displacement of attention from those who most need affirmation. Or, at the other extreme, God is enrolled as a member of the society of the needy.

True, believers and unbelievers alike experience difficult times. Even the most simple and natural aspirations, such as getting married and having children, have become disproportionately difficult and elusive. The option of suicide reveals that for many the cost-benefit analysis of life has become overwhelmingly negative. The consumer culture tends to enclose us in a mood of calculation and introspection. And when everything has its price, who can afford to pay? If there is no free lunch for anyone, we become suspicious of gifts, even the uncanny gift of existence. When our problems and our needs seem to be our all, and when we consider the fact that we are all affected by ailing institutions—in government, academe, church, and market—then praise seems to be a flight of fancy. When we experience a kind of cultural Black Death, survival appears to be the key value.

The matter becomes more poignant when expressed in religious terms. The violence, the bloodletting, and the sheer scope of our human failures this century past—and our complicity in such evils—conspire to make the praise of God sound escapist indeed. How can we praise God? How dare we praise God? If God has been acting, what are his achievements? Surely not *this* present state of our world! And if God is powerless to act, how can he be deserving of our blessing?

To put the matter so bleakly provokes its own kind of questions. Are we missing something essential to our Christian existence? Has our horizon so contracted in depression that we feel a personal as well as a cosmic numbness? Under the dark ceiling of human projections, are we so closed within the windowless walls of our pressured lives that the heights, lengths, breadths, and depths of the mystery giving itself to fill and illumine our lives can barely be recognized? Although we are God's creation, and although Christ has come to save us, we live as if we are nothing more than creatures of our own making, and so left to save ourselves.

A religion might work, of course, if it dulls the aching nerve of life. But if it does, there is little joy and wonder in that—especially if we find ourselves living in an economy of scarcity, competing for finite and nonrenewable resources. Indeed, the ever-renewable resources of God's grace are beyond us. It would seem that the biblical heart of stone has solidified within us as a heavy, cold, numb, lifeless lump. The heart of flesh, lifting in the energies of hope and praise, simply does not beat with the warm blood [of] a larger life. Thus, we each have to ask ourselves whether and to what extent we have concentrated all the mystery of the universe into our own irritable calculations. Have we, in fact, become so radically self-centered that God occurs in our lives only as a screen onto which we project our own dissatisfaction and bitterness? Has the expanding universe of grace been replaced by our pitifully shrinking world?

I would suggest that thanksgiving and the praise of God should pervade the whole scope of our lives and being. Sometimes it is simply ecstatic, a spontaneous act of Christian *joie de vivre*. At other times, it is a defiant act wrung from our depths of suffering and hope, born of a determination to acknowledge that even in darkness God does not cease to be our light and our life. Whatever the circumstance, God and only God stands at the beginning and at the end of all we are—and thanking the divine goodness is a permanent dimension of the faith, hope, and love we profess. It is not as though God needs our praise and thanksgiving, however, for it is ourselves who need to become thankful and praising people if we are to live in our true freedom and spiritual creativity. The fourth weekday preface expresses this point in a sturdy logic: after acknowledging before God "that we do well always and everywhere to give you thanks," it goes on to state two vital considerations:

> You have no need of our praise,
> yet our desire to thank you is itself your gift.
> Our prayer of thanksgiving adds nothing to your greatness,
> but makes us grow in your grace....[12]

In the fragmentation and threat we experience in our world today, the eucharistic imagination takes us out of ourselves so that we can find our real origin, center, and destiny in God. Although personal or global miseries work to depress our minds and enclose us in a sense of general defeat, praise and thanksgiving—gifts of grace—are signs of a transformed heart. Our hearts expand to be more than the sum total of the evils we either suffer or contribute to. Our acts of praise and thanksgiving are not so much an affirmation of God as one who is in need of our recognition, but more our willingness to enter into the unfailing joy of Christ (see John 16:22–24; 17:13). God, in all and despite all, is *God*, the "light [in whom] there is no darkness at all" (1 John 1:5). By glorifying God, we live out the God-ward direction of our lives. Insofar as we begin to rejoice that God alone is God—that the Father who is infinite light, life, and love has revealed himself in Christ—we enter into the pure unselfishness of the communal life of the Trinity itself and participate in the selfless love of the divine

Persons. In the midst of life's pressures, our praise of God rises as a prayer that the name of the Father will be hallowed, that his kingdom will come, and that his saving will may be done on earth as in heaven.

In this way, praise is our way into the inner life of God. By resolutely refusing to live enclosed in a world made up of problems—being in the wrong place at the wrong time—we live in the infinitely larger universe that God is bringing into being. There, in that larger universe, our *thinking* is not restricted to problemsolving from our own limited resources but becomes a *thankingthinking*—to borrow a phrase from the German philosopher, Martin Heidegger. Through thanksgiving, a life restricted to mere calculation becomes an existence alive with contemplation. And even while we struggle to find an answer to the problems that beset us, we now address them in the light of the limitless grace of a God, the one to whom we pray, who alone can save us. Praise and thanksgiving lift us beyond the world of our needs to acknowledge the uncanny gift of existence and the further grace of salvation—and the Giver from whom all gifts come:

> *Through him you give us all these gifts.*
> *You fill them with life and goodness,*
> *you bless them and make them holy.*[13]

In the presence of this divine giver, Christian existence becomes a hymn of praise:

> *Through him,*
> *with him,*
> *in him,*
> *in the unity of the Holy Spirit,*
> *all glory and honor is yours,*
> *almighty Father,*
> *for ever and ever.*[14]

The great *Amen* that follows this doxology at once sums up the eucharistic attitude pervading Christian life and suggests the open God-ward horizon in which it is to be lived out in the midst of the fragility and challenges that confront us. Through this eucharistic conversion to praise and thanksgiving, our lives are defined not by some endless list of problems but by the mystery of love that is our origin, our sustenance, and our destiny. Although Paul is imprisoned and soon to be executed, his eucharistic imagination breaks out in the counsel he gives to the Colossians:

> Let the word of Christ dwell in you richly; teach and admonish one another in all wisdom; and with gratitude in your hearts sing psalms, hymns, and spiritual songs to God. And whatever you do, in word or deed, do everything in the name of the Lord Jesus, giving thanks to God the Father through him (Colossians 3:16–17).

The Christian becomes finally a "singing self" in the great polyphony of creation.[15] The Eucharist expresses this transformed self as a conversion to mind and heart. The Church prays: "We come to you, Father, with praise and thanksgiving through Jesus Christ your Son" to "offer you this sacrifice of praise for ourselves and those who are dear to us."[16] The connection of this eucharistic ("thankful") attitude to "sacrifice" implies a continuing effort to go beyond the self-enclosed patterns of our existence to acknowledge our true center, the source from which all the gifts of creation and redemption have come.

Eucharistic Conversion: Love

The Eucharist awakens our faith to the real presence of God's love. The divine "being-in-love" is the ultimate life form given to transform our human existence: "So we have known and believe the love that God has for us. God is love, and those who abide in love abide in God, and God abides in them" (1 John 4:16). In the Eucharist, God is present to us as love and we are present to that love, dwelling in it, imbibing it, and being transformed by it. We know this love as it is actualized in the self-gift of Jesus himself: "We know love by this, that he laid down his life for us" (1 John 3:16). God has "so loved the world" (John 3:16) as to give what is most intimate and personal to himself, his Son, for the our salvation. The Son, revealing and communicating the loving character of the Father, expresses this love by loving "his own who were in the world" and loving them "to the end" (John 13:1f). The Son's self-sacrifice for others becomes, in turn, "the way, and the truth, and the life" for those who believe in him (John 14:6), and his disciples are those who have heard his new commandment "to love one another as I have loved you" (see John 13:34).

The Eucharist embodies God's love in the reality of our earthly existence and draws believers into the "love life" of God himself which, of its nature, is endless and eternal. The Word is with us not only through the Incarnation but also in the eating and drinking basic to our communal existence. The love that God is has given itself to be eaten and drunk as the sustenance and form of eternal live. By communicating to us the "love life" of the Trinity itself, the Eucharist expresses the expanding outreach of the divine life: "Those who eat my flesh and drink my blood abide in me, and I in them" (John 6:56; see also 15:4) Our dwelling in Jesus and his dwelling in us derives from the living communion existing between the Father and the Son: "Just as the living Father sent me, and I live because of the Father, so whoever eats me will live because of me" (6:57). The love that sent Jesus into the world is the same love that now sends his disciples forth in their mission of love: "As you [Father] have sent me into the world, so I have sent them into the world" (17:18). When the original unity of the Father and the Son opens itself to the world, it works to enfold of all believers, present and future, into a perfect unity: "that they may be [perfectly one]" (v. 23); "that they may all be one. As you, Father, are in me, and I am in you, may they also be in us" (v. 21).[17]

The intense consciousness of mutual indwelling and communion which the Eucharist suggests can only be understood in terms of two great desires. First is the desire of Christ that we might be where he is: "Father, I desire that those also, whom you have given to me, may be with me where I am, to see my glory, which you have given me because you loved me before the foundation of the world" (John 17:24). Each eucharistic celebration is the outcome of the unfailing prayer of the glorified Jesus. Even though this sacrament is celebrated within the pilgrim history of the Church— a real presence contending with a real absence—each eucharistic event occurs as the Father's answer to Jesus' desire, "that they may be one, as we are one" (John 17:11).

Corresponding to and, indeed, resulting from this prayer of Christ is the second desire: the desire of the Church for the return of the Lord. In proclaiming "the death of the Lord until he comes" (1 Corinthians 11:26), the Eucharist gives expression to the Church's desire for its love to be consummated in definitive union with its Lord: Maranatha! "Come, Lord Jesus!" (Revelation 22:20; see 1 Corinthians 16:22). The Eucharist expresses the desire that Jesus will enter fully into his own, establishing his Lordship, filling all things, bringing all things to completion in a transfigured universe. In the meantime, the Eucharist is celebrated in adoration and longing, in an expectant openness to the mystery of ultimate love at work, as we "do this in [memory] of me" (Luke 22:19).

As the memorial of Christ's love, the Eucharist is saturated with the deepest expressions and experiences of love: desire, union, mutual self-giving, the ecstasy of self-sacrifice for the other's good, the self-nourishing being of the beloved other—all such aspirations of love are woven into the texture of the sacrament of Christ's presence. It is not a matter of individual devotion or mystical experience, but something dealing with the most radical character of life itself and of the fulfillment of all creation. The living, loving mystery of God gives itself to be the life of the world, the love life that is the food and drink of our being, to be literally eaten and drunk, tasted and felt, heard and seen (see 1 John 1:1–4).

The eucharistic imagination understands the real presence of Christ only in terms of a "being-in-love" that is beyond all the conditions and reservations that this world imposes. In this it must appear as folly to a culture in which the experience of love has been so drastically disenchanted and so physically trivialized. Still, the imagination inspired by the eucharistic form of love contests all cultural attempts to reduce love to mere consumption. It expresses in our world the unrealizable excess which every true form of love obscurely recognizes. For this sacrament of Christ's self-giving love is an emblem of the passion, both in the sense of what Christ suffered and of the passion that impelled him to love his own "to the end" (see John 13:1). In him, the lover's extravagant rhetoric becomes a statement of real life: "My flesh is true food and my blood is true drink" (John 6:55).

The love that the Eucharist embodies challenges the psychic numbness that is born of disillusionment and the defeat of love both in the world at large and in the Church itself. The passion and fundamental physicality of the Eucharist shocks our tendency to reduce spirituality to the domain of bloodless, disembodied, unfeeling, and isolated pure spirits. As the source and apex of the activity of the Church, the Eucharist is the singular instance of "our hearts burning within us while he was talking to us on the road," and how he makes himself known to us "in the breaking of the bread" (see Luke 24:32, 35). It is the realization of love in its final and most lasting form: "Love never ends" (1 Corinthians 13:8).

Conclusion

The eucharistic imagination is released in a conversion of mind and heart. To be involved in the Eucharist is to participate in a "holy and living sacrifice." It demands that we move beyond the defenses and isolation of individualism into a "holy communion" that, potentially, will exclude no one. It means exposing ourselves to searching the truth of Christ's presence that leaves no one individual, nor any Christian community, undisturbed. Praise and thanksgiving flow from the humble acknowledgment that we exist and live and move forward only through the ceaseless flow of divine gifts. Finally, the Eucharist draws us into a universe of love filled with the passion of God to awaken the world to its true life.

These dimensions of eucharistic conversion give a radical orientation to the life of Christian hope and prayer. From the earliest times, the Eucharist was celebrated as a literal "orientation," as the worshiping community turned toward the rising sun as a symbol of the risen Christ.[18] Such a tradition of "facing east" has a contemporary relevance, as we welcome a new millennium. In the surprises and challenges that lie in store, each Eucharist anticipates a future determined not by human ingenuity or failure, but by the gift of God. It strains forward to welcome him who died and rose and will come again, as he rises out of the depths and fills creation with his radiance.

∾ 7 ∾
EUCHARISTIC IMAGINATION
AND HOPE

I n proclaiming the death of the Lord until he comes (see
1 Corinthians 11:26), the Eucharist is the sacrament of hope.
In the antiphon for the feast of *Corpus Christi*, Saint Thomas
Aquinas catches this hopeful, forward-looking movement as it is
nourished on the memory of Christ's Passion and the present experience of grace:

> O sacred feast in which we partake of Christ: his sufferings
> are remembered, our minds are filled with his grace and we
> receive a pledge of the glory that is to be ours.

The Eucharist inspires images of the future in the light of the
past and in the reality of the present. The Christ who is to come is
already really with us—and so the Christian imagination is released to express in word and deed what no human eye or ear or
heart can immediately grasp of "what God has prepared for those
who love him" (see 1 Corinthians 9). The manner in which Christ
gives himself to us in the eucharistic bread and wine anticipates
the fulfillment of all creation in God—"God...all in all"
(1 Corinthians 15:28). Hope for what we are, individually and
collectively, is affirmed in Christ, for "in Him every one of God's
promises is a 'Yes'" (2 Corinthians 1:20).

Understood in this way, the Eucharist is an antidote for fun-
damentalist fantasies about the future. What is to come, the "last
thing" (*eschaton*), is celebrated in familiarity of what, by the gift
of God, is already present. For the Eucharist makes "really present"
what God has in store, and our future comes home to us in this

actual community. As for all who make up the Church, it is popu-
lated by people inescapably aware of limitation and imperfection
in themselves and others. In this regard, the Eucharist envisions a
future that is more than the salvation of pure spirits. In the same
way, it works against a narrowly individualistic kind of hope. For
it is the celebration of a community not as shades haunting the
world but as sharing food and drink in its midst. When Christians
celebrate their hope in this manner, they are not engaging in private meditation, nor are they meeting for a philosophical discussion on the afterlife. Rather, they are eating, drinking, tasting,
breathing, and sharing the real presence of the future that God
has prepared for them in Christ.

Hope Against Hope

As a corrective to an overly poetic or visionary understanding of
the eucharistic imagination, it is as well to remember that Jesus
exercised his imagination in the most familiar of all human contexts, namely the sharing of a meal involving the most common of
commodities: bread and wine. Moreover, he did this in the most
unpromising of situations. His disciples were full of foreboding
for him and for themselves; one of them actually would betray
him and the rest would abandon him. Those who were determined
to purge their world of the imagination that Jesus embodied joined
in the conspiracy to do away with him. Yet, in the teeth of such
terminal opposition, in the face of failure, and in vulnerability to
the forces ranged against him, Jesus surrendered himself to the
Father's will for the sake of all who would follow him—and who
would experience, in their own time, a world inhospitable to everything the Eucharist represented. For him as for them, there was
no question of putting a nice construction on a fundamentally
violent and ugly reality. Rather, there was only a witnessing to the
ultimate power of a love that would transform everything. However long it would take and whatever the cost, the love of Christ
was intent on changing the world from top to bottom.

Hope for the Whole

In the Eucharist, Christ is present as hope's food and drink. He is the final form into which the whole universe is being drawn. The decisive, all-embracing significance of the mystery of Christ appears in the various Pauline and Johannine statements: all things are made through him, in him, for him (see John 1:3; 1 Corinthians 8:6; Colossians 1:16). He is both at the origin and at the end of what is coming to be; he is the one to whom all things are tending; he is the image in which all things are made. So utterly does Jesus fill all dimensions of the universe that Paul understands that universe as "all things holding together in him" (see Colossians 1:17). As the coherence of all creation, Jesus both unifies and reconciles, embodying the Father's outreach toward a fragmented and alienated creation: "For in him all the fullness of God was pleased to dwell, and through him God was pleased to reconcile to himself all things...making peace by the blood of his cross" (Colossians 1:19f). All these metaphors of causing, containing, unifying, and reconciling aim to express how Christian hope finds its center and support in the Incarnation, death, and Resurrection of Jesus Christ.

Christ is above, before, and beyond all creation. Because he is the Word, the unique Son of the Father, and the Lord of all, it is not the world that utters or produces or contains him. For he is God's all-creative Word, producing and containing everything that exists. Nonetheless, because he precedes and exceeds all created reality, he is "within" the universe in a special manner. On the one hand, he is with God in the beginning, is identified with God (see John 1:1–2), and all creation came into being through him (v. 3). On the other hand, this Word has become flesh, dwelt among us (see v. 14) and, lifted up on the cross, draws all to himself (see John 12:32). Believers are thus attracted to him in the "flesh" of creation.

From different points of view, Jesus embodies God in the midst of creation while, at the same time, he embodies creation in the sight of God. To merely human eyes, he is "in the world," immersed in its cosmic processes and acting within its history. But, to the horizon of hope, the universe is "in Christ," finding in him its ultimate life and transformation. On him hinges the door that lets God into our world and opens that world to God.

Creation originates in Christ—and it is condensed and fulfilled in him. Such a sense of God's creative action characterizes the hope of the Church through the course of history. As a gathering of believers, it is a distinguishable presence in the world. In its faith and hope, the Church is that part of the cosmos that has awoken to the mystery pervading all creation, a visible witness to the invisible grace that is at work. United in the Spirit of Christ, the People of God are themselves the sacrament of the Body of Christ being formed to its fullness as history unfolds and reaches toward its goal.

All the activity of the Church is sacramental; through the ages, the Church bears Christ within itself and witnesses to his presence. It is "Christopher-ic," literally, "Christ-bearing." The presence of Christ is actualized in our lives in the seven sacraments celebrated in the course of Christian life.

However, these sacraments, and even the Eucharist itself, would be empty signs if they were disconnected from the basic sacramentality of the Church. Moreover, even the sacramental nature of the Church would be without substance if it were separated from the great cosmic sacramentality of creation in which the whole Christ is being born: "We know that the whole creation has been groaning in labor pains until now" (Romans 8:22). God is at work through all time and space so that Christ "might be the firstborn within a large family" (v. 29). Creation itself would be going nowhere unless, at its heart, there blazed the all-transforming mystery of Christ. Even then, the mystery of our transformation in Christ would be little more than a mythological expression unless it were an outflow from the self-giving love of the Trinity itself: "God is love, and those who abide in love abide in God, and God abides in them" (1 John 4:16). The Father expresses his love by giving his only Son (see John 3:16) and by giving everything into his hands of the Son (see John 13:3). The Son responds in love by clinging to nothing of his own but by surrendering all to the Father (see John 4:34). The Holy Spirit witnesses to this love by drawing all into the self-giving relationship that exists between the Father and the Son (see 1 John 4:13; 5:6–7).

Eucharistic Hope

The eucharistic imagination weaves together many meanings into the texture of Christian hope. It connects so many mysteries: Trinity and Creation, the Incarnation, death, and Resurrection of Jesus, the gift of the Spirit, and the Church with all its sacraments. Still, familiar earthly realities, bread and wine—the fruit of the earth and work of human hands—ground and earth the meaning of the Eucharist, even as they are charged with immense new significance. We are, therefore, dealing with an intensely compact symbol of what Christian hope is about.

The play of the eucharistic imagination works on this charged, compact reality. Saint Thomas Aquinas, for example, carefully positioned his theology of the Eucharist by appreciating it first of all as a "sign" of God's gift.[1] Because the Eucharist is the sign of Christ's free self-giving relationship to the Church, he is present to us in a way that exceeds all worldly categories. The term Saint Thomas Aquinas used for this unique mode of presence was *transubstantiation*.[2] God's action changes things, beyond the scope of any earthly form of change. This Spirit-wrought transformation changes the bread and wine into the body and blood of Jesus Christ, thus serving as an answer to the prayer of the Church to the Father, the creator of all:

> *And so Father, we bring you these gifts. We ask you to make them holy by the power of your Spirit, that they may become the body and blood of your Son, our Lord Jesus Christ, at whose command we celebrate this eucharist.*[3]

For the bread and wine to become the body and blood of Christ implies that such a "becoming" is a result of that great transformation that occurred when the Word-became-flesh, and when his suffering humanity was transformed in the resurrection from the dead. To forget this is to forget that the Eucharist is primarily a sign of the total mystery of God's redeeming love at work.

Unfortunately, the impression is too often given that the transformation of the eucharistic bread and wine is a strange, even arbitrary, miracle isolated from God's love for all creation. But if the eucharistic change is taken in isolation, the bread and wine are simply the "matter of the sacrament," the "raw material," as it were. As a result, the change that occurs—transubstantiation—is simply a replacement of one substance with another, even though the "accidents" remain.

The spiritually unnerving aspect of this is that the reality (the real presence) of Christ is imagined as ousting the reality (the substance) of the created earthly realities. The heavenly Christ is crudely imagined as coming from the "outside," from "beyond" our world, to replace the basic reality, the "inside" of the realities we know and use. When matters are imagined in this way, the remaining appearances of the bread and wine are thought of as a kind of shell and temporary camouflage of Christ now present to us. But Jesus' real presence in the Eucharist demands a price: the abolition of some part of created reality. Although the Eucharist is certainly held "to contain" the heavenly Christ in a mysterious fashion, the earthly realities of bread and wine are emptied of their deepest reality—that is, their substance.

While not denying the intense realistic thrust of such a theology, I believe it can be expressed in a way more apt to do justice to the presence of the risen Lord among us. In this perspective, the real presence of Christ can be understood not as though he were "contained" in the eucharistic elements, but more in that the bread and wine are "contained" in Christ in a new and final manner. The reality of Christ does not so much supplant the realities of the bread and wine but, rather, enables these elements of creation and human culture to attain their fullest reality in him. By being transformed into his body and blood, the bread and wine are not less than they were previously, but fully and finally what they are meant to be: "For my flesh is true food and my blood is true drink" (John 6:55).[4]

To appreciate this point, we must keep in mind the relationship of Christ to the whole universe, as mentioned above. For in Christ "all things hold together," just as he "sums up" all creation (see Ephesians 1:10). He is the "firstborn" of all creation and its final homecoming. He draws into himself creation in all its forms. In this extended sense, all of creation is on its way to being "transubstantiated"—transformed in Christ to achieve its final reality.

The critical issue here is that Christ's relationship to creation is not tyrannical. For his grace "heals, perfects, and uplifts" all created nature. Christ gives a completion and perfection beyond anything imaginable.[5] The words of *Gaudium et Spes* point in this direction:

> Christ left to his followers a pledge of this hope and food for the journey in the sacrament of faith, in which natural elements, the fruits of man's cultivation, are changed into His glorified Body and Blood, as a supper of brotherly fellowship and a foretaste of the heavenly banquet (§38).

Then, there is an even larger implication for Christian hope, especially if we remember that the production and sharing of the bread and wine used in the Eucharist represent a number of values related to human creativity, collaboration, and community, as *Gaudium et Spes* also points out:

> When we have spread on earth the fruits of our nature and our enterprise—human dignity, brotherly communion, and freedom—according to the command of the Lord and in his Spirit, we will find them once again, cleansed this time from the stain of sin, illuminated and transfigured, when Christ presents to his Father an eternal and universal kingdom (§39).

The eucharistic transformation, then, implicates all the elements of nature and culture, and it involves the whole cosmos and the universe itself. It affects our appreciation of the physical world and regards all forms of life as well as the distinctive life of human consciousness. It presupposes the value of our cultural creations and the different ways the Spirit has been at work throughout history. All these, says *Gaudium et Spes*, are destined to find their fulfillment in Christ:

> The Word of God, through whom all things were made, was made flesh, so that as a perfect man he could save all men and sum up all things in himself. The Lord is the goal of human history, the focal point of the desires of history and civilization, the center of [humankind], the joy of all hearts, and the fulfillment of all aspirations. It is he whom the Fa-

ther raised from the dead, exalted and placed at his right
hand, constituting him judge of the living and the dead. Ani-
mated and drawn together in his Spirit we press onwards on
our journey towards the consummation of history which fully
corresponds to the plan of his love: "to unite all things in
him, things in heaven and things on earth (Ephesians 1:10)"
(§45).

To celebrate the Eucharist within such a comprehensive vision is to realize that the transformation of the "fruit of the earth
and work of human hands" into the body and blood of Christ is,
in fact, the anticipation of a universal transformation; the transformed bread and wine anticipates the radical transformation of
all creation. In Christ the transformation and fulfillment of the
universe is already in progress.[6] In the Eucharist, what we offered
as bread and wine—as products of nature and human culture—
are given back to us bearing their final "christened" form. By eating and drinking this "true food" and "true drink," Christian hope
expands to cosmic proportions. Its "holy communion" has now
to include all creation, in which hope is hope for the whole.

For bread and wine are not abolished by the Spirit's action.
Rather, these familiar elements of our earthly life are constituted
in their ultimate significance—food and drink communicating to
our humanity nothing less than life unending. The eucharistic food
is no longer the "food that perishes, but…the food that endures
for eternal life" (John 6:27). The Eucharist is the "true bread from
heaven" (John 6:32)—the "bread of God…that…gives life to the
world" (v. 33). The "bread of life" (v. 35) nourishes us with the
life-giving reality of Christ—"and the bread that I will give for the
life of the world is my flesh" (v. 51). Through the transforming
action of the Spirit, the eucharistic elements are no longer mere
nutrients of biological life ("not like that which your ancestors
ate, and they died" [v. 58]), but the food and drink of eternal life.
By eating and drinking what Christ gives us, we have a foretaste
of life in a transformed universe.

Foretaste of Eternal Life

As the sacrament of hope, the Eucharist not only imagines but *tastes* what is to come. The language of taste is deeply biblical. Believers, for example, "have tasted the heavenly gift, and have shared in the Holy Spirit, and have tasted the goodness of the word of God and the powers of the age to come" (Hebrews 6:4–5). The psalmist exhorts us to "taste and see that the LORD is good" (Psalm 34[33]:8). In the sacramental realism of eating and drinking the body and the blood of Christ, our spiritual taste is heightened and intensified. Saint Thomas Aquinas remarks on the appropriateness of the metaphor of tasting related to God's presence:

> One experiences a thing by means of sense, but the experience of a thing present differs from the experience of something absent. One experiences a distant reality by sight, smell, hearing. Whereas one experiences a present reality by touch and taste. Still, while touch attains this present reality in an extrinsic way, taste attains what is present in an interior way. Now God is neither distant from us nor outside us…and so the experience of the divine goodness is called tasting.[7]

In the eucharistic meal, we taste the object of our hope already present to Christian faith and love. Our hope is given new eyes to envision the future and a new hearing to catch the ultimate promise of the Word that is spoken. As it inhales the Spirit—the atmosphere of the new creation—eucharistic hope tastes not death, but the reality of eternal life. In the earthiness of the sacrament, our hope has a fundamental contact with its future as it handles the tokens of a transfigured creation. It eats, drinks, and savors eternal life, to relish in anticipation the heavenly banquet.

∽ 8 ∽
ECOLOGY AND THE EUCHARISTIC IMAGINATION

The ecological well-being of our planet is one of the pressing concerns of our day, bringing to the surface many complex problems aching in the depths of our modern lifestyles. How can a respect for nature find its proper place in our technologically driven culture? Must human culture always be at the expense of the natural world? Is that natural world only preserved by banishing the human presence as destructive and parasitical? Here we explore the manner in which eucharistic imagination suggests its own ecological vision by bringing nature and culture together in a way that respects both by relating them to the incarnate, eucharistic reality of Christ.[1]

Nature, Culture, and Eucharistic Reality

In the eucharistic perspective, the real presence of the whole Body of Christ is communicated to us through the transformation of the shared "fruit of the earth and the work of human hands." The bread we offer becomes for us the "bread of life," and the wine we bring becomes "our spiritual drink." In this way, the Eucharist is a celebration of both the holiness and wholeness of creation, which appears as holy in that the earthy elements that sustain our lives and communication have such a central place in the eucharistic gift. Unless creation was radically from God, it could not figure so largely in God's relationship to us. Moreover, the Eucharist underscores the wholeness of creation; matter, life, and the human spirit are connected in the one God-created universe, where the fruits of nature and the work of human creativity are integrated in the deeply cosmic sense of how God communicates himself to us in Christ.

Nature and the history of human creativity interpenetrate. The produce of the earth, for example, is instanced in the wheat and the grapes. The productions of human creativity are exemplified in that the grain and the grapes are made into bread and wine. The expressiveness of human culture appears in the manner in which such food and drink are used in the convivial communication of our meals and festive celebrations. Further, the eucharistic meal embodies Christ's self-gift. In its turn, Christ's self-giving incarnates the love of the Father himself: "For God so loved the world that he gave his only Son, so that everyone who believes in him may not perish but may have eternal life" (John 3:16).

The Eucharist brings together all these gifts and all these forms of giving, to draw us into a universe of grace and giving. From nature's giving, we have the grain and the grapes. From the giving of human work and skill, we have the gifts of bread and wine. From the giving of family and friends flow the gifts of good meals and festive celebrations. From Jesus' self-giving at the Last Supper, the disciples are given his body and blood as the food and drink that nourishes their union with him. He breathes into his disciples the gift of the Spirit. And working in and through all these gifts and modes of giving is the gift of the Father, who so loved the world. When the Church celebrates the Eucharist, all these gifts come together to nourish Christian life with the gift of God.

The fourth eucharistic prayer invokes the Father as the luminous source of the universe:

Source of life and goodness, you have created all things
to fill your creatures with every blessing
and lead all men to the joyful vision of your light.[2]

This prayer, while expressing a sense of all creation as a divine revelation, highlights our human task in relation to the world. Because we are made in God's image, we realize that image by caring for what God has created:

Father, we acknowledge your greatness:
all your actions show your wisdom and love.
You formed man in your own likeness
and set him over the whole world
to serve you, his creator,
and to rule over all creatures.[3]

In this hope-filled task, faith looks to a final transformation of the universe:

Then, in your kingdom, freed from the
corruption of sin and death,
we shall sing your glory with every creature
through Christ our Lord,
through whom you give us everything that is good.[4]

The Eucharistic Vision

As the artificiality of technological culture has uprooted us from nature, our world today is threatened with ecological disintegration. We sense that we are not humbly *a part* of nature but, rather, are set violently *apart* from it. In this ambivalent situation, the Eucharist is a resource for a more humble and far-reaching wisdom.[5] As inspiring an appreciation of the whole of creation, the Eucharist is the primary example of "Catholic" imagination, in which *kat'holou* ("openness to the whole") is understood in its full communal and inclusive sense. Such an inclusive imagination envisions a totality in which each part lives in the whole, and the whole is present in each part. It brings home to our faith, in the time and space of our existence, that God was in Christ "reconciling *the world* to himself" (2 Corinthians 5:19, emphasis added). It leads toward a "holy communion," excluding no one and nothing of what God has loved into being.

The eucharistic gift of Christ's body and blood has the effect of restoring our sense of being creatures of this earth and stewards of God's good creation. To praise and thank the Creator is to cherish and care for creation. The most intense moment of communion with God is at the same time an intense moment of our communion with the earth. For the "fruits of the earth and the works of human hands" are not magically vaporized by the action of the Spirit; rather, they come into their own as the nourishment for life unending. Put most simply, in the idiom of John's Gospel, the bread and wine become "true food and...true drink" (John 6:55).

"Transubstantiated" in this way, the sacramental elements of the Eucharist anticipate the cosmic transformation that is afoot, not as something that leaves the created cosmos behind but as promising its healing and transformation.

Such a positive vision is one of the important ingredients that Christian faith can offer to ecological awareness. Our day is marked with an increasing appreciation of the diversity of life and a concern to protect the unique wonder of our biosphere. But something more than a purely rationalist calculation is needed. If there is to be a conservation of the nonrenewable resources of our planet, the ever-renewable resources of faith, hope, and love must be involved. Further, the eucharistic perspective looks beyond a naive ecological ideology, with its tendency to regress to an idealized past as an unspoiled and innocent state. On the other hand, doctrinaire evolutionary ideology tends to empty the significance of the present into an impersonal and incalculable future, so that both the past and the present have value only in terms of what they are evolving into. Here, too, eucharistic faith provides a more generous framework; it envisions the God-given future actually occurring within our earthly and historical time. Thus, everything is not deferred to a future that is indifferent to what we now are. Our earth, our flesh, and our blood matter to God's creative purpose. We are not being emptied of what we are, for we are fed with the bread of heaven and filled with the energies of the Spirit in the flesh and blood, in the food and drink of our present existence.

The great emancipations of the modern age have had to pay a particularly heavy price. In the struggle against what was perceived as oppressive tradition or archaic order or biological limitation, such forms of liberation have also left so much behind. The modern emancipated individual, for example, is uprooted from any sense of nature, for nature meant only limitation and threat. Individual freedom became detached from any sense of a sacred nurturing universe. Since that larger, englobing mystery of things was outside the range of human control, freedom was not a matter of surrendering to the greater mysterious whole, but of defining oneself against it and apart from it.

The Enlightenment, therefore, had its costs. To the degree that human culture was willing to pay, the range of universal connectedness was lost in the exchange. Mircea Eliade remarks:

> As for the Christianity of the industrial societies and especially the Christianity of intellectuals, it has long since lost the cosmic values it still possessed in the Middle Ages. The cosmic liturgy, the mystery of nature's participation in the christological drama, have become inaccessible to Christians living in a modern city...at most we recognize that we are responsible to God and also to history—but the world is no longer felt as the work of God.[6]

When we can no longer feel that the world is the work of God, an extreme alienation results. Nonetheless—and this is what Eliade does not grant—there remain ever-renewable resources of Christian vision and sensibility, and these resources typically are found expressed in the Eucharist. In a more "enlightened" Enlightenment, they can be retrieved, but this time in a way that will be less rationalistic and individual, and more attuned to our immersion in nature and our cosmic connectedness. A cosmic connection was, indeed, part of the deep sensibility of Christian tradition—as any familiarity with the great medieval doctors, Saint Thomas Aquinas and Saint Bonaventure, clearly shows. But now, with the loss of that sense of connection, the world has been regarded more as a big resource engine to be harnessed and exploited, its products consumed for our varied versions of individual self-fulfillment.

The modern mind, even that of the Christian believer, needs to be reimmersed in the cosmic whole. Neither a return to ancient science nor a rejection of modern achievements are acceptable alternatives. But what is required is a larger and more humble reinterpretation of the traditional declaration of Ash Wednesday, citing Genesis 3:19: "You are dust, / and to dust you shall return." Now, however, the character of that dust can be understood as a cosmic reality; we are made of stardust. Our bodies are distillations of the cosmic matter and energies that make up the physical

universe over the billions of years of its emergence. We are embodied in a cosmic totality.

The Christening of the Universe

We usually apply the hallowed term *transubstantiation* to the
manner in which the bread and wine are changed into the Lord's
body and blood. As has already been mentioned in the previous
chapter, we are still in need of a larger cosmic perspective, however,
for the mystery of the Eucharist is set within a cosmic process of
transformation.[7] The physical, the chemical, and the biological
structures of our universe have culminated, through a succession of
transformations, in human consciousness. In our minds and hearts
the universe has become aware of itself as a vast and wonderful
mystery. Before it and within it, we live and breathe, humbly aware
that we are not the center or origin of all this great happening. We
are thankful for the sheer gift of our existence, and we are patient
and hopeful as it moves us on toward some final outcome.

If the great world of nature has brought us forth, we exist
now as spiritual beings, capable of thinking, acting, loving, hop-
ing, and praying. We arise out of nature, but we are not contained
by it. For now there is an even larger span: the openness, the creativity, and the freedom of spirit and soul. We can respond because we
possess the freedom to live in a spiritual horizon and so to determine the direction of our lives. At the very least, we experience
our marvelous, unfinished, and restless humanity as a question:
Are we to live on the earth, enjoying what it offers and suffering
through what it imposes only to die in a state of spiritual uncon-
sciousness? What's more, is the question of the origin and goal of
all this gift too big or too threatening to ask? Who or what is the
giver of all these gifts? Are we to take our existence for granted,
understanding ourselves, in the end, as mere consumers, even on a
cosmic scale?

On the other hand, however, we are capable of asking: Do we
owe our existence to Something or Someone, the great Creative
Mystery that has brought us into being? Are we to live on this
earth, through which we have been given so much, yet have no
responsibility to be part of the giving—as life-givers, love-givers,
caregivers?

To be in any way disturbed by these kinds of questions is to find ourselves living on a horizon alive with wonder about our origins, our responsibility, our destiny. If the universe is creation, what does its Creator intend for us? What are we to do with ourselves as the stream of life lifts us up, carries us on, and confronts us with the fact that we have not been here nor will be here forever? The span of human history (two hundred thousand years?) and the eight decades or so of any given life are only the merest instant in the fifteen thousand million years that have gone into the making of our world. And yet, "We are nature's big chance to become spirited."[8]

For a eucharistic faith, the spiritual scope and shape of humanity is uniquely expressed. It presupposes all the material and biological transformations that peak in the emergence of human consciousness, carrying forward the momentous leap in human history that occurred in Israel's special covenant with the One God. Then, Mary's Spirit-inspired "Let it be with me according to your word" (Luke 1:38) embodies the genetic potential of creation as she gives her consent to become pregnant with the Christ, the final "life form" of creation. The Christmas antiphon so aptly expresses: "Let the earth be open to bud forth the savior!" Under the action of the Holy Spirit, this woman of Israel brings forth Jesus, the Christ, the Son of God, into life on this planet. His love unto the end on the Cross, and the transformation that occurs in his Resurrection, draws creation into the field of Trinitarian life: "[May they be one], as we are one" (John 17:22). While the longing of the human spirit opens to a horizon filled with the self-giving love of the divine mystery itself, the searching and hope of the human spirit is met with the action of God's own Spirit, forming us and our world into the Body of Christ.

As the Spirit animates our humanity with the life of the Incarnate Word, Christian faith blossoms into its sacramental imagination; symbols, gestures, words, relationships, and biological processes of our world come to be appreciated in different sacramental contexts as "visible signs of invisible grace" (Saint Augustine). In the Eucharist, these elements reach their most intense and comprehensive. There, the risen Lord takes fragments of creation—the elements of our earthly reality that nature and history have combined to produce—to transform them into something more, in anticipation of a new totality: "This is my body; this is my blood."

Throughout history, Jesus' transforming identification with the matter of our world has been continued as the Eucharist is celebrated: "Do this in memory of me." By receiving the eucharistic gift of his body and blood—by responding to the Lord's invitation to connect with the cosmos as he has done—we are, in fact, claiming this world as our own in the way that Christ already possesses it. Thus, we become immeasurably larger selves in a world of divine incarnation. We are not here commending some vague form of pantheism, but recognizing the reality of the Incarnation itself as it makes us see the world as the "body" of God.[9] By assuming our humanity, the divine Word necessarily makes his own the world and universe to which that humanity is essentially related.

Eucharistic Contemplation

Both Greek philosophy and Hebrew faith strongly distinguished between God and the world, between the Creator and creation. The distinctively Christian faith in the Incarnation, the Word-made-flesh, is celebrated in the Eucharist. It invites us to bring together what even the deepest philosophy and the greatest faith had hitherto kept apart.

The sacrament of the Eucharist implies that God is so much God, so infinite and creative in goodness, that the divine presence reaches into the innermost depths of matter to give the physical world a part in communicating the most divine of gifts. From another point of view, the material world is so much deeply and fully created by God, so possessed and held in being by the Creator, that it is the medium through which the divine mystery reaches out to us: "The Word became flesh and lived among us" (John 1:14). The sacramental imagination of the Church affirms, in fact, that not only bread, wine, water, oil, and human gestures figure in the sacraments but also our human sexuality—as in the sacrament of marriage. When the Eucharist and the other sacraments celebrate the intimacy of God present and working in creation, this is far from being a regression to mythological thinking. Rather, it is a recognition of the Incarnation, inviting us to appreciate how the universe comes into being through the Word and finds its coherence and full reality in him: "He was in the beginning with God. All things came into being through him, and without him not one thing came into being. What has come into being in him was life, and the life was the light of all people" (John 1:2–4).

The range of Christian faith is always expanding. The great mystics witness to the indwelling intimacy and extent of God's presence in the universe.[10] In their sense of the utter otherness of God, contemplatives first undergo a purifying withdrawal from the created world. But their detachment is preliminary to openness and surrender. An example of this "way of negation" are the words of John of the Cross: "Nada...nothing, nothing, nothing... and even on the mountain, nothing."[11] Beyond all human conceptions, images, and projections, faith experiences a kind of spiritual nakedness before the all-surpassing mystery—God alone. To pray is to enter into this "cloud of unknowing"; it attends to "a sound of sheer silence" (1 Kings 19:12) and leads to emptiness. The praying believer must be "nakedly intent" on the divine will and surrendered to that will, lost in it alone, beyond the tiny clamor of needs and manipulation.

But then follows the illumination. In going up the mountain of ascent, we meet the Other coming down into the plains of creation. God is ever creating the world—and ourselves within it—to make us hear his Word more fully and to receive his Spirit more fully. To Philip's request, "Lord, show us the Father and we will be satisfied," Jesus asks in his turn, "Have I been with you all this time, Philip, and you still do not know me? Whoever has seen me has seen the Father" (John 14:8f). But even this "seeing" discloses perspectives beyond the scope of human vision and control. There is a play of darkness and light: "If I do not go away, the Advocate will not come to you; but if I go, I will send him to you" (John 16:7).

In this play of absence (the earthly departure of Jesus) and presence (his return through his gift of the Spirit), we begin to know our place for the first time. Christ's presence to us is disclosed as truly real—in the concrete earthly reality of the world into which the Word has come in the flesh and to which the Spirit is sent. Jesus promises, "I will do whatever you ask in my name, so that the Father will be glorified in the Son. If in my name you ask me for anything, I will do it" (John 14:13–14). In Christian prayer, creation awakens to its original mystery, a point that has been teased out in the words of a man of faith who is also an outstanding poet as he reflects on Jesus "praying in a certain place" (Luke 11:1):

> When Jesus prayed and taught us to pray, he was doing two things. He was entrusting himself to the Begetter of the universe, and he was giving himself to his brothers and sisters throughout time and space. What we call the Our Father, or the Lord's Prayer, faces at once into all that has ever surrounded and determined the fortunes of the human race, and into the lives of individual men and women. It frames an act of confidence in the goodness of God who made and makes us, it articulates our shared need, and it declares a resolve to be creative on behalf of others. The name of the "certain place" of prayer is, in other words, "Compassion." In that country of the mind and heart, one sees that our universe is not an anonymous indifferent milieu, but the homeland and heartland of God. And at the same time, one sees that God the life-cherisher calls all of us to be life-cherishers and life-givers in concert with him. We ask for food and forgiveness, because we need them both. We agree to offer food and forgiveness, because others need them both. If we mean what we say, prayer will send us back, a little shaken but more than a little heartened, to the tasks of everyday....The country of Compassion can be, and should be, wherever we happen to be.[12]

The Father's house is a home of "many dwelling places" (John 14:2). Even as we live and breathe in this world, we can still follow Jesus into our particular "dwelling place," as we pray and open our hearts to God's goodness revealed in all things. In the depth and breadth of our prayer, we find the universe to be "not an anonymous and indifferent milieu, but the homeland and heartland of God."

Admittedly, our world can appear to be "anonymous and indifferent," as scientists tell of its enormous space and the billions of years that have gone into its making. The disciplined objectivity of science, after all, is intent on delineating the structure of the physical universe and speaking in idioms that can easily make human beings feel that their presence here is purely the result of blind impersonal chance. But the scientific productions of the human mind achieve a strange outcome when they leave no room for the human heart. Science would hardly be a success story, for example, if it prevented us from appreciating the wonder of the cosmos as the "homeland and heartland" of God, and of the human spirit. It would be an odd turn in scientific endeavor, indeed, if it insisted that scientists, human beings like us all, had to define themselves out of the cosmos they so impressively explore.

A genuine science can hardly ignore the most obvious and astonishing phenomenon: human consciousness itself. If it gave way to a purely materialistic bias in the name of dispassionate objectivity, if it insisted on ignoring the reality of spirit and its destiny, it would confine us in a world without fundamental meaning and value. The scientific mind might somehow haunt the immense complex universe, but would hardly inhabit it. We would be left with a world without persons.

In contrast, a eucharistic imagination gives a deeper sense of mystery to the impersonal "objectivity" of science. It brings to the scientifically imagined universe a sense of itself as being a divine creation and an incarnation. It is a space of communication where God has called us into being. The Father has sent his Son to dwell among us, and the Holy Spirit makes us aware of this great mystery at work. The Word of God is in our midst in the Incarnation, making our sufferings his own through the cross. Ultimately, his resurrection from the dead inspires in us even now the hope of a final universal transformation.

By nourishing us with such mysteries, and bringing them home to our minds and hearts, the Eucharist celebrates the universe as a great spiritual breathing space. In that God-filled space, everything and everyone is related. The eucharistic universe does not suffocate the life of our world; rather, it is immeasurably hospitable to all that we are. In this regard, the Eucharist educates the imagination, the mind, and the heart to apprehend the universe as one of communion and connectedness in Christ. That totality is materialized in the earthly, physical elements of the shared bread and wine of the sacrament, in the community of believers receiving it, and in Christ giving himself to them as their food and drink. Faith experiences the universe as in a process of being transformed into a new creation.

Through the Eucharist, the whole is now offered to be reclaimed as belonging to Christ, and to all who are "in Christ." In eucharistic imagination, the universe is imagined "otherwise." Contemplative faith lifts and brings together the superficial, the fragmented, the alienating elements in our experience into another vision. The universe—"Christened," seeded with the Spirit-energies of faith, hope, and love—is being transformed (transubstantiated) into the Body of the Risen One. To this hopeful vision, the Body of Christ becomes the milieu of our existence, in which nothing is left out, nothing is left behind.

Christ's Real Presence to the Real World

Thus eucharistic faith envisages our existence in the world as an indwelling in shared mystery. It invites us to see our world charged with communication as a great field of relationships to everything and everyone. Although we human beings have been busy through our short history in sundering our relationships to one another, to creation itself, and to the God himself, the divine Word has been writing our collective name in the dust of the earth we share. For "in Christ"—according to the Pauline vision—"all things hold together" (Colossians 1:17) and are gathered up in him (see Ephesians 1:10). Through the "image of the invisible God," he is "the firstborn of all creation" (Colossians 1:15). All things are made "in him," and are destined to be "for him" (v. 16). The mystery of Christ is for the universe the all-unifying attractor, the direction inscribed into its origin, the goal drawing it onward, and the force holding it together. All reality—the physical world, all forms of life, the distinctive life of human consciousness, its cultural creations, and its transformation in the Spirit—is embodied in the plenitude of the Risen One. As the heart and center of a transformed creation, he is the life and the light of the world (see John 1:3–4).

Through the eucharistic imagination, a distinctive ecological vision and commitment take shape. If the literal meaning of *Eucharistia* is "thanksgiving," the comprehensive meaning of such thanksgiving is found in our gratitude for all the kinds of givings and gifts that nourish our existence, and the self-giving love of the Father is the origin: "In this is love, not that we loved God but that he loved us and sent his Son to be the atoning sacrifice for our sins" (1 John 4:10). Paul begins his Letter to the Ephesians with a great eucharistic outpouring:

> Blessed be the God and Father of our Lord Jesus Christ, who has blessed us in Christ with every spiritual blessing in the heavenly places, just as he chose us in Christ before the foundation of the world to be holy and blameless before him in love....With all wisdom and insight he has made known to us the mystery of his will...as a plan for the fullness of time, to gather up all things in him, things in heaven and things on earth (Ephesians 1:3–4, 8, 10).

In our day we are coming to appreciate how the Father's original love has worked in an amazing providence. The "one God and Father of all, who is above all and through all and in all" (Ephesians 4:6), is ever at work for our sake, gathering up all things in Christ, the "things of heaven and things of earth." Whether our gaze is upward to God or downward to the earth, we are confronted with so many dimensions of God's giving. We are, indeed, "up to our necks in debt."[13] Divine providence has guided the great cosmic processes over billions of years to create the conditions in which planet Earth could be a biosphere, a place of life. The same providence has worked through the evolutionary dynamics that have made us what we are: "earthlings," human beings co-existing with a million other forms of life in the delicate ecology of this planet. In this continuing chain of giving and receiving, we live not only with but "from" and "off" and "for" one another. The long history of gifts, the creative providence of God's acting on our behalf, has led to the Word of God being present to us in person. The Word becomes flesh and dwells among us to bring healing, forgiveness, and abundant life. His cross reaches into the depths of the evil we suffer or cause to promise reconciliation in an always greater love.

Finally, his Resurrection is our assurance that this long history of creative love will not be defeated. Indeed, love and life will have the last word—beyond anything we can imagine. The crowning gift of the Spirit is made to guide us into all truth, as he declares "the things that are to come" (John 16:13).

So much has been given to us that we might exist and live. How, then, do we begin to repay what we owe in a noninflationary currency? How do we, too, become a life-giving influence in return? How do we act in this economy of giving and grace?

The eucharistic command of the Lord, "Do this in memory of me," arises from the imagination of one who gave himself in his whole being for the sake of the many and the all. By entering into the spirit of Jesus' self-giving, we begin to have a heart for all God's creation, refusing to leave out of our concerns no aspect of that good creation that the Creator has loved into being. By entering into Christ's imagination and becoming members of his body, we are, in fact, putting our souls back into our bodies. For we become re-embodied in him who is related to everything and everyone. In him and through him, we co-exist with all creation. We begin to live in a new time frame determined by the patient, creative goodness of God, who is working to draw all things to their fulfillment. We start to have time, beyond the pressures and compulsions of instant demand, to appreciate the wholeness of God's creation. We begin to own, as truly our own, what we had previously disowned or bypassed—above all, our living solidarity with the world of nature.

The eucharistic imagination thus stimulates its own ecological perspectives. Everything has its part in God's creation; everything has been owned by the divine Word in the Incarnation; everything is involved in the great transformation already begun in his Resurrection. We are bound together in a giving universe, at the heart of which is the self-giving love of God: "Unless a grain of wheat falls into the earth and dies, it remains just a single grain; but if it dies, it bears much fruit" (John 12:24). We are living and dying into an ever larger selfhood to be realized in a network of relationships pervading the whole of the universe and reaching even into the Trinitarian relationships that constitute the very being of God.

The Eucharist, then, inspires us to welcome, with a more generous hospitality, the great, generative reality of the cosmos and the ecological reality of our planetary biosphere, and belong to both in a larger spiritual space. For all this has its place in the "Father's house of many dwelling places" (John 14:2).

To obey Jesus' command, "Do this in memory of me," implies, then, a re-membering of all that has been dismembered in the sterile imagination of our culture. The eucharistic forms of faith, hope, and love do not allow either our universe or even our planet to be left behind. Spiritual progress is not a spiritual escape from what we are, but a generous reclamation of the physical world, so that it is neither forgotten nor abandoned to absurdity, despair, or defeat. We cannot set nature aside, for it is our own flesh and blood. Loving our neighbor means loving the whole cosmic and planetary neighborhood in which we exist. In the measure we taste and celebrate the charged eucharistic reality of Christ's presence to us, the Christian imagination expands to its fullest dimensions—and Paul's prayer begins to be answered:

> I pray that you may have the power to comprehend, with all the saints, what is the breadth and length and height and depth, and to know the love of Christ which surpasses knowledge, so that you may be filled with all the fullness of God (Ephesians 3:18–19).

The time and space of our earthly existence are filled with the energies of true life. Here and now, we are destined not only to be jubilant participants in the feast but also, through all the giving and service that life and love demand, to be part of the meal. We are called to contribute the energies of our lives to the great banquet of the new creation. With Jesus, we fall as grains of wheat into the holy ground to die, in order not to remain alone (see John 12:24). Such a sense of life suggests a deeper understanding of nature and, indeed, of our earthly existence. The earth itself begins to appear, in the words of Beatrice Bruteau, as

> ...the Eucharistic Planet, a Good Gift planet, which is structured in mutual feeding, as intimate self-sharing. It is a great Process, a circulation of living energies, in which the Real Presence of the Absolute is discerned.[14]

The eucharistic imagination envisions the world "otherwise," in its deepest and most hopeful reality. The sacrament of Christ's body and blood nourishes our minds and hearts into a sense of ecological wholeness. It cures our imagination from the egotistical illness, to offer it the healing sickness of a more generous belonging to all. The need for this salubrious nourishment is expressed in the words of Einstein:

> A human being is part of the whole, called by us the "universe," a part limited in time and space. He experiences himself, his thoughts and feelings, as something separated from the rest—a kind of optical delusion of his consciousness. This delusion is a kind of prison for us, restricting us to our personal desires and to affection for a few persons nearest to us. Our task must be to free ourselves from this prison by widening our circle of compassion to embrace all living creatures and the whole of nature in its beauty.[15]

The relational existence that Christ nourishes inspires a sense of reality at odds with any individualistic vision. In expressing his eucharistic relationship to us and our world, Jesus is acting out of his own sense of reality as a field of communion and mutual indwelling. He prays "that they may all be one. As you, Father, are in me and I am in you, may they also be in us....I in them and you in me, that they may become completely one" (John 17:21, 23). Our unity in God derives from the way the Father and the Son are united in the one divine life. In other words, the divine persons are not independent entities somehow managing to come together. Rather, divine life is an eternal flow of one into the other, in relationships of mutual self-giving: "Instead of taking as the norm of Reality those things which are *outside* one another, he [Jesus] takes as a standard and paradigm those who are *in* one another."[16] Here we are challenged to imagine our inter-relationships in terms of mutual indwelling modeled on the union existing between the Father and the Son. We nourish the other into being—and the life-giving nourishment we give is nothing less than the gift of ourselves. We are "in" one another for the life of the other. By being from the other, for the other, and so, *in* the other, our earthly human lives participate in God's own Trinitarian love life.

The eucharistic imagination inspires a deep ecological sensibility in which our ways of relating to everyone and everything in God's creation occurs within a field of shared life and communion. The first movement of Christian existence is to give thanks (*Eucharistia*) for the wonder of the love that has called us to be part of a commonwealth of life. Such "thanking" deeply conditions the "thinking" necessary to address the urgent ecological problems of our day. Obviously influenced by eucharistic symbolism, a noted ecologist writes:

> To live, we must daily break the body and shed the blood of creation. When we do this knowingly, lovingly, skillfully, reverently, it is a sacrament. When we do it ignorantly, greedily, clumsily and destructively, it is desecration. In such a desecration, we condemn ourselves to spiritual, moral loneliness, and others to want.[17]

Although we have no intention of reducing the eucharistic celebration of the mystery of the Lord's death and resurrection to ecological concerns, still, the Eucharist does affect such concerns. It sustains the vision and the hope necessary to address the urgent problems confronting the human race at the beginning of this new millennium. A conscience formed by the Eucharist works against the powerful cultural tendencies to desecrate God's good creation. The sense of universal communion the Eucharist inspires works against the spiritual and moral loneliness that threaten our culture. The heartlessness that shuts out the poor and the needy from the great house of life—and proves incapable of valuing anything except in terms of immediate usefulness and economic reward—is exposed to a redeeming influence. In all parts of the planet, in the daily round of millions of lives, the Eucharist is celebrated. The communities concerned with this celebration awaken each day to a corporate rededication of themselves not only to sharing the bread of life with the hungry, not only to compassionate involvement on behalf of the suffering, but also to a commitment to the ecological well-being of the planet itself. Through this sacrament, faith can come to see the earth as a living sacrament of God's loving presence.

Through its eucharistic imagination, the Church can be an

inspirational force for those who have come to appreciate planet Earth as *Gaia*, a wondrous, varied, delicate living system. Christians are representatives of

> ...humanity becoming more fully integrated with the being of Gaia, more fully at one with the presence of God. It is a deepening into the sacramental nature of everyday life, an awakening of consciousness that can celebrate divinity within the ordinary, and, in this celebration, bring to life a sacred civilization.[18]

Christian faith moves through time—but always walks on holy ground. The challenge to bring to life a "sacred civilization" is being felt today with special urgency.

Conclusion

Some might feel that religious symbolism is one thing, while the conflicts and strategies of practical ecological concerns are quite another. I can only suggest that the movement toward a richer and more inclusive life begins with a new way of imagining the world. Great symbols orientate us within the living wholeness of reality and give us both the passion and patience to grapple with it. Here I have offered a reflection on the Eucharist as a primary symbol within the life of Christian faith. It is an essential expression of the poetry of such faith, unfolding as it does in a universe of grace. The eucharistic imagination radically reshapes our experience, to make the unseen and unspoken glow with significance, even if the struggle to have words for such matters remains.

As the source and goal of the whole life of the Church, the Eucharist relates us to Christ, connects us with one another, and reembodies us within the life of planet Earth. It opens into a horizon of religious, communal, planetary, and cosmic belonging. Our universe is being drawn into the trinitarian life, toward that ultimate point at which "God may be all in all" (1 Corinthians 15:28).

ᖇ 9 ᖇ

THE EUCHARIST AND
THE HOLY SPIRIT

The Eucharist is not only the sacrament of the life-giving presence of Christ but also the most significant indicator of the action of the Holy Spirit. As the "Lord and giver of life," the Spirit stirs within all creation, "groaning" in labor to bring to birth the fullness of Christ. Saint Paul imagines the divine Spirit "groaning" in the "groanings" of Christian hope to open it to its fullest dimensions:

> We know that the whole of creation has been *groaning* in labor pains until now; and not only the creation, but we ourselves, who have the first fruits of the Spirit, *groan* inwardly while we wait for adoption, the redemption of our bodies. For in hope we were saved....Likewise the Spirit helps us in our weakness; for we do not know how to pray as we ought, but that very Spirit intercedes [for us with unutterable *groanings*] (Romans 8:22–24, 26, emphasis added).

The celebration of the Eucharist in the context of fragility and ambiguity of any Christian community can be realistically related to the "groaning" presence of the Holy Spirit in our midst. Leading up to the words of consecration, the priest prays for the Spirit to transform the bread and wine: "And so, Father, we bring you these gifts. We ask that you may make them holy by the power of your Spirit, that they might become the body and blood of your Son, our Lord Jesus Christ...."[1] And then, immediately after the consecration, the same Holy Spirit is invoked on those who are about to receive the Eucharist gift: "Grant, that we, who are nourished by his body and blood, may be filled with his Holy Spirit, and become one body, one spirit in Christ."[2]

The Gospel of John presents the coming of the Spirit as the "advantage" following the completion of Jesus' earthly mission. Although Jesus no longer will be with his disciples in the usual pattern of worldly relationships, he will be with them through the Spirit he sends them from the Father (see John 16:7). The Paraclete will abide with and in his disciples (see John 14:17), calling to mind everything that Jesus had previously communicated (see John 14:26), so to expose the violence, lovelessness, and false glory of the world (see John 16:8–11).

In the ongoing life of the Church, the Eucharist is the privileged site in which the presence and action of the Spirit are most clearly discerned. Through the sacramental signs, the Spirit of truth brings us into contact with the full reality of Christ—Jesus Christ, who has come in the flesh and has given himself on the cross for the life of the world. His resurrection indicates both the triumph of God's love and the most vivid form of the eternal life it promises: the "things that are to come." To read Jesus' words in a eucharistic context is to appreciate the key role the Spirit, as the "other Paraclete":

"I still have many things to say to you, but you cannot bear them now. When the Spirit of truth comes, he will guide you into all truth; for he will not speak on his own, but will speak whatever he hears, and *he will declare to you the things that are to come*. He will glorify me, because he will take what is mine and declare it to you. All that the Father has is mine. For this reason I said that he will take what is mine and declare it to you" (John 16:12–15, emphasis added).

Thus the Holy Spirit acts through the Eucharist to bring home to believers ever fuller dimensions of the reality of God's love for us in Christ. Guided by this Spirit, we eat and drink the "things that are to come." The Spirit of truth enables us to nourish our hope on the "true bread" and the "true drink" that are the body and blood of Christ (see John 6:55). On the cross, Jesus "bowed his head and gave up his spirit" (John 19:30) to the new family of God, represented in Mary and the Beloved Disciple (see 19:25–

27). When the soldier pierced the side of the dead Jesus with the spear, the disciple witnessed to the blood and water that gushed forth. From the heart of the Crucified flow the waters of baptism and the blood of the Eucharist. As the Spirit works, these sacramental gifts will continue to bathe and nourish the Church through the ages: "The Spirit and the water and the blood, and these three agree" (1 John 5:8). The Eucharist, we might suggest, is the high point of such "agreement," as the Spirit guides the baptized to find in Christ the food and drink of eternal life.

As the Spirit continues to be invoked with transforming effect in every Eucharist, we are given an understanding of how God works. In any Spirit-wrought transformation, the reality of the world, the history of the world, and the identity of human agents are not annihilated or replaced. Rather, when the Spirit breathes, all reality comes to its fulfillment in Christ. As the ancient axiom has it, "grace heals, perfects and elevates nature." The Father sends his Spirit not to overwhelm either our human identity or, more generally, the reality of the created world. Rather, under the Spirit's guidance, creation finds its homecoming and fulfillment in God. As Jesus declared, "In my Father's house there are many [rooms]" (John 14:2).

In other scriptural contexts, the same principle is apparent. In the Spirit, Jesus is conceived, anointed, and empowered. Possessed by the Holy Spirit, he preaches, heals, and drives out evil spirits. Yet in no way is his humanity, or that of anyone else, downplayed or compromised. In fact, the various temptation accounts underscore the conviction that Jesus' mission entailed no escape from the human condition (see Matthew 4:1–11; Luke 4:1–13; Hebrews 2:18; 4:15). Under the influence of the Spirit, the humanity of Jesus expands, as it were, into solidarity with the suffering and the lost; his humanity is all-embracing. He gives himself in the totality of his body and blood "for many" (Matthew 26:28)—an inclusive phrase correctly translated in the eucharistic prayers, as "for you and for all."

In the light of this very same Spirit, the Church celebrates the Eucharist. It is not only an inspired recollection of the passion of Christ but also a "pledge of the glory that is to be ours." For the Holy Spirit has acted in bringing about the resurrection of the Crucified, in which Jesus is glorified in his identity as Son of the

Father, and as brother to all. As the Spirit acts in Christ, the "Lord and giver of life" is the agent of a universal resurrection. Human identity is not destroyed but expanded to its fullest and most final form:

> If the Spirit of him who raised Jesus from the dead dwells in you, he who raised Christ from the dead will give life to your mortal bodies also through his Spirit that dwells in you (Romans 8:11; cf. 1 John 3:2).

The Spirit of resurrection now forms the community of the Church into the body of Christ (see Ephesians 1:22). In this new vital embodiment, each one possesses a special gift and vocation: "To each is given the manifestation of the Spirit for the common good" (1 Corinthians 12:7). In this Spirit-led communion, each Christian can say with Paul, "It is no longer I who live, but it is Christ who lives in me" (Galatians 2:20a). We are liberated in our liberty—"You were called to freedom" (Galatians 5:13)—and enjoy a unique sense of personal worth: "I live by faith in the Son of God, who loved me and gave himself for me" (Galatians 2:20b).

From these different points of view, the Eucharist is the most intense point in the field of the Spirit's universal activity, and the Christian imagination is stimulated to an ever-fresh appreciation of how the Spirit is acting to "Christen" all creation. We become aware of the manner in which the "real presence" of Christ and the "real presence" of the Spirit are related. God's saving action is condensed in Christ, but only to expand further through his Spirit. Jesus gives his Spirit, and the Spirit leads to Christ. The eucharistic prayers call on the Spirit to make Christ really present by transforming the bread and wine. The gifts we offer—"the fruit of the earth and the work of human hands"—represent all the hopes hidden in our earthly existence: our hope for peace, community, and lasting life. On these the Spirit is invoked, first, "that they may become the body and blood of your Son, our Lord Jesus Christ"; and, then, "that we, who are nourished by his body and blood, may be filled with his Holy Spirit, and become one body, one spirit in Christ."[3]

A meditation of Saint Catherine of Siena helps us catch the

eucharistic imagination in flight. In this dialogue, the Father speaks to his children:

> I am their bed and their table. This gentle loving Word is their food, because they taste the food of souls in this glorious Word and because he himself in the food I have given you: his flesh and blood, wholly God and wholly human, which you receive in the sacrament of the altar, established and given to you by my kindness when you are pilgrims and travelers so that you may not slacken your pace because of weakness nor forget the blessing of the blood poured forth for you with such burning love, but may be constantly strengthened and filled with delight as you walk. The Holy Spirit, my loving charity, is the waiter who serves them my gifts and graces.
>
> This gentle waiter carries to me their tender loving desires and carries back to them the reward of their labors, the sweetness of my charity for their enjoyment and nourishment. So, you see, I am their table, my Son their food, and the Holy Spirit who proceeds from me, the Father, and from the Son, waits on them.[4]

Thus Christian hope grows among those made one in Christ and his Spirit. The Church prays that Christ may "make us an everlasting gift" to the Father and that we may "share in the inheritance of [the] saints."[5] However fragmented our world or dismembered our various communities, the Eucharist nourishes our hope. Taking into ourselves the food and drink of eternal life, we are taken out of ourselves by the Spirit of Christ to breathe the free air of a new creation: "Everything old has passed away; see, everything has become new!" (2 Corinthians 5:17).

☙ 10 ☙
EUCHARISTIC TIME:
THE DAY OF THE LORD

hristian faith has always made its own accommodation of the third commandment, "Remember that thou keep holy the Sabbath Day." Not the last, but the first day of the week was to kept holy, in memory of the Lord's Resurrection. Justin Martyr offered this explanation to a non-Christian audience in the Rome of the second century:

> On the day called Sunday there is a meeting in one place of those who live in the city or the country and the memoirs of the apostles or the writings of the prophets are read as long as time permits. Then we all stand up together and offer prayers. And when we have finished the prayer, bread is brought, and wine and water, and the president similarly sends up prayers and thanksgivings to the best of his ability, and the congregation assents, saying the Amen. The distribution and reception of the consecrated elements by each one takes place, and they are sent to the absent by the deacons...We all hold this common gathering on Sunday, since it is the first day, on which God transforming darkness and matter, made the universe, and Jesus Christ our Savior rose from the dead on the same day.[1]

This Christian way of keeping time inspired a particular social and cultural conduct in line with the Jewish Sabbath tradition. For example, as a way of affirming the radical dignity of even the most lowly, servile work was forbidden, for all human beings had a God-given destiny. Church law insisted that the oppressed laborer had a day's gift of leisure. Today, in these modern times of long weekends, Sunday selling, and all the variety of sporting and recreational opportunities, the complexity of our current ways of structuring time forces us to rethink the long tradition of respecting and keeping a holy day. The pastoral expedient of the Saturday vigil Mass is one example—but that hardly ends the matter. The question keeps coming up: Has the pressure of modern life so squeezed the weekly span of our lives that there is no room for "abundant life" (see John 10:10)? Are holidays, for instance, really *holy* days?

Free Time?

A feature of our present experience is the extreme preoccupation that has entered into our experience of time. With the ever available distraction of instant electronic entertainment, and our lives being filled with constant demands, too often we feel as if there simply is not enough time. We have an enormous number of choices to make at any give time—and each one demands its own energy. But the sheer number, variety, and urgency of these choices threaten to swallow up our basic freedom and make our ways of relating to one another hurried and superficial. As a result, the fundamental ability to determine who we are and what we really want is eroded. It is as though we are so engrossed in admiring and buying all the offerings of the supermarket that we forget to eat; and so gradually lose both the taste for a decent meal and the skill to prepare it. The only freedom on the freeway is to go faster than usual—if it is not rush hour—to get to our destination more quickly, leaving any friendly exchange a perilous distraction in the onrushing traffic. So we saved time—but for what?

Time, even in this era of longevity, has become a precious commodity. We live longer, but we don't seem to have more time. In the midst of so many competing claims of work, family, and "leisure" activities, time is so organized, measured, structured—in a word, so already "taken"—to the point that we begin to feel about time in a new way. It is an unrenewable resource that seems to be so little "ours," yet so much a part of what we are and want to be. We are most what we give time for, just as we find ourselves most through those who have time for us.

Although our time is precious, it is also our most familiar enemy. It hurries us on, aging our bodies and exhausting our energies. Yet it is also slow—so much so that it takes a long time to grow, to learn, to come to some kind of wisdom, to become what we want to be. Although we are privileged to the instant communication of world events, our lives are both informed and burdened with tragedies and disillusionment on a global scale. So much is happening that we live in a psychic jet-lag that saps our capacities either to lay hold of the present or imagine the future. Stressed by the present, shocked by the future, we move further from any nurturing or familiar past.

Time seems to be merely spending us, wasting us with its unrelenting passage and leaving us without either patience or hope. We are like passengers who suddenly have been told that the train we boarded is now an express service to the end of the line—making no stops in between. It leaves us helplessly gazing out of the window as our intended station flashes by. We can't get off, and we don't want to stay on—the familiar panic of an anxiety dream.

Lost Time?

As the aeons roll on, a great impersonal process empties the present of any fullness and robs our world of any resting place. In this state of constant movement, there is no homecoming to some promised familiar place, only the endless movement to…where? We begin to sense that everything we most treasure is caught in the lottery of a blind evolutionary advance into what is both beyond our ken and outside our control. Time becomes demonic, an obscure, unfeeling force that has no time for us.

Given this, we are forced to reappraise what time means and how we are spending it. How can we keep time holy? How is there room for any Sabbath? How can such time be holy? And if it is holy, how can it be kept holy? How can it be appreciated in any wholeness beyond a mere succession of meaningless moments? Basic questions, indeed—and, ironically, demanding further precious time to hear and answer them. Such questions take us to the point of faith, and only at that point can we make any sense of a commandment to keep a Sabbath.

Time Saved!

The weekly Eucharist enables us to re-member time because it situates us in a time of grace. At this point of faith, we can adore God as the Creator and Goal of a time-structured world. By becoming flesh, the Word has entered time, and God acts within time and history. That time and that history can be treasured as God's way of having time for us. The divine Spirit, after all, has time for creation. God's creative power is at work in the slow emergence of the cosmos, beginning with the Big Bang of fifteen billion years ago that brought about this time—and ourselves within it. God has time for our history by inspiring its unfolding through all its eras and epochs. Indeed, the Creator has taken time over our making.

In the Sabbath spirit, we are invited to appreciate our time as holy; to surrender to it as the unfolding of providence; to welcome it all as grace; to bear with it as the patience of God. God is now with us, as this present moment, emerging from an immemorial past, moves into the incalculable future. There, God will be our end, bringing to completion the mortal, stuttering groping of the world's ways, for "Jesus Christ is the same yesterday and today and forever" (Hebrews 13:8). He is God's mark on time, the fullness of time bringing the past, the present, and the future together: "Christ has died, Christ is risen, Christ will come again!"

Time becomes holy when we begin to have time for God in the way the Giver of all gifts has time for us. For, at its deepest level, time is the gradual display of a gift that our humanity cannot receive or appreciate all at once. Creation unfolds in accord with the timing of an eternal love. There is no instant creation; there are no instant people; and because God has taken such time over us, we, too, must make time to recognize the divine patience and acknowledge its generosity. There can be no creation and no final salvation without time. All divine gifts come in time.

The Time of Our Lives

To the degree that we recognize this simple fact, time unfolds as God's gift of grace. Each year is the "year of our Lord," as each century and millennium is the temporal form of God's love for us and the whole time-bound world. In our disappointment or frustration with the way things have gone for us, we might fantasize about escaping to another time, in the past or the future, or perhaps to some "timeless" point from which we can let the world pass us by. But faith brings us back to this moment: "Now is the acceptable time"—an essential moment in the long unfolding of the way God has taken time over our creation and salvation.

To dwell in time in this way is to find our own times to be the "best of times." This moment is full of the eternity of love. This moment—now—is where God is to be sought, served, and welcomed. When time is received as God's gift, there can be no utterly bad times. Even though time imposes its different patterns of growth and decay, of progress and decline, of health and sickness, of peace and unrest, all this is part of the timeliness of God's grace. Our times are holy.

Still, the holiness of time is only possessed in the heart. In that deepest center of our selves, the successive instants of time are distilled and formed into a gracious story; a whole story and a holy story. We have to make time for the holiness of time if we are to live its deepest direction and promise. Making time and having time for the holiness of time is just another name for what we do in the Eucharist. In the liturgy, we enjoy "free time" in the deepest sense. Within the Eucharist, we don't just mark time in a kind of directionless inactivity; rather, we center ourselves in the eternity that holds time together. The restless, jumbled succession of moments come together in an unfolding story of grace, of "grace upon grace" (John 1:16), of grace that keeps on being grace— even now.

And *even now* is the key point; grace has timed itself to include this irrepeatable moment. But the timeliness of grace presupposes that we are making time to recognize it. Thus, time spent over the Eucharist is time well spent.

By resisting any version of ourselves as "instant" people, we celebrate the eucharistic Sabbath, the day of rest and peace. Being still in God—spending time together in celebrating the mysteries that are disclosed in God's good time—is itself the most freeing time. Our personal and communal life of prayer hallows time by giving time to the One who has had so much time for us. We give time to holy time.

I am reminded of an old Egyptian custom of stopping the clocks when the house was entertaining guests. Although the host and guests knew that time kept moving, they were aware that the hours and minutes were no longer to be measured by ordinary routines. Rather, a deeper current of life was allowed for during time in which guests were welcomed and entertained. The Sabbath of life is like that: when the Lord has found time to visit us, time begins to mean something different and thus is no longer measured by the clock of our calculations but by the gift that has been made.

The interior hallowing of time, in the Jewish and Christian tradition, is always set within a history of grateful memory and future hope. More to the point, the traditional obligation of the Sunday Eucharist insists that we make time for God in the company of one another, as a period of time given in appreciation of a great historical visitation. For the Eucharist nourishes believers into a sense of belonging together in Christ, as a pilgrim people passing through time together. Carrying within itself the mysteries of the Incarnation, life, death, and Resurrection of Christ, time draws us into one shared history. It bears the news of a victory and promises a universal homecoming. The Eucharist celebrates the real presence of Christ as the one who is present in every moment of our journey through time. He has redeemed the times—for time is no more an empty succession of anxious, pointless moments in the separate lives of countless individuals. What is in the making, what is growing through time, is for the building up of the body of Christ "until all of us come to the unity of faith and of the knowledge of the Son of God, to [the measure] of the full statue of Christ" (Ephesians 4:13).

Eucharistic Time

The Eucharist educates us to have time in Christ. In giving thanks, we reach back only to turn forward. For our times unfold in the presence of the Mystery that has come forth in the fullness of time to gather all into itself. We are not endlessly seeking to recapture the past; rather, impelled by that past which bears the life, death, and Resurrection of Christ Jesus, we turn toward a future in which our destiny will be completed and fulfilled. The future is not an impersonal, dispassionate evolutionary process, but a movement into God, to the one who will be "all in all" (1 Corinthians 15:28). Each celebration of the Eucharist is timely, forming time into its wholeness, redeeming our times, promising a divinely destined outcome.

True, the pressures of the present, the sheer driven-ness of the moment, can make the Eucharist seem like a waste of time. The heavenly banquet, however, is remote from the world of fast food; the culture of instant gratification and control is allergic to the bread of life. Those who allow themselves to be enclosed in the demanding succession of present moments have nothing to be thankful for, and thus suffer the loss of both memory and hope. But, by keeping this day holy, there is a remedy for the disease of the instant. Time is healed, made whole, and finds its depth and direction. The span of time opens to include the God who has had time for us—and has taken time over our making. When our time is measured by God's time, boredom and futility are challenged by the surprises of the Spirit. And the Father waits to welcome us into a house of many rooms.

This is to suggest that going or not going to Mass is not a simple matter of individual choice. Rather, the decisive consideration turns on whether we choose to be publicly part of Christ's way of imaging the goal of time and the God-given promise and direction that our history bears within it. Radically, it is a question of having time for what really matters, or wasting time and the gifts it contains. To absent ourselves from the Eucharist is to deprive the Church of our presence and to lessen its time-saving mission in the world. A bishop of the early Church hit the nail on the heard:

Exhort the people to be faithful to the assembly of the Church. Let them not fail to attend, but let them gather faithfully together. Let no one deprive the Church by staying away; if they do, they deprive the Body of Christ of one its members.[2]

EPILOGUE
EUCHARISTIC IMAGINING

We have come together
around this table under the sign of the cross of Jesus,
full of the memory of what he has done for us.
We now pray to become most fully what he calls us to be.

For he is the Yes to all God's promises,
the Amen to all our prayers (2 Corinthians 1:20).

He has opened our minds to understand the Scriptures;
for in him the law of Moses,
the words of the prophets
and the prayers of the psalms
are now fulfilled (Luke 24:44).

The Word, read and spoken,
resonates with the promise of life for the world,
for our healing, our nourishment, our joy.
In him and through him,
from the many gifts you have given us,
we offer to you, God of glory and majesty,
this holy and perfect sacrifice,
the bread of life and the cup of eternal salvation.

Blessed are you, Lord God of all creation!
Through your goodness we have this bread to offer,
which earth has given and human hands have made.
May it become for us the bread of life.

The bread which earth has given—
which we have received from the silent, fertile soil—
this wholesome bread nourishing our lives with energy
and health.

It is the bread of this earth—
the earth we cultivate, mine and plunder—
the wide earth over which we trace our paths
    and make our journeys.
This silent earth bathed in morning light,
    this beautiful planet,
a tiny thing in the teeming galaxies of space,
but warm and well-lit for us,
generous, faithful, ever surprising,
a homeland.

This secret bountiful earth is our field
    and space of life.
Billions of years have gone into her making.
The strong winds and rushing waters
have shaped and carved her over uncounted years,
as she is washed by the rain,
torn and healed by the play of all the elements and seasons,
all her colors lively and beautiful under the light of the sun.
Mother earth, keeper of many secrets,
showing many moods and faces:
hard rock, lush plain, cold mountain,
deep jungle, desert, oasis,
playground and battleground,
farmland and wasteland,
uncomplaining beneath pick and plough,
faithful, hospitable earth,
wonderland of imagination,
homeland of all we are.

The meager seed of our possession is tossed on the earth,
wagered in the strange lottery of life.
The sowing waits on the harvest,
in surrender and in hope,
waiting on life, growth, and ripeness....
We wait on the time; we wait through the seasons.
Amen to the times;
Amen to the seasons;
Amen to the dying and the new life beginning,
to damp and dry,

to decay and to renewal,
to the work and the waiting....

Now springs the joy of the first growth.
The fields quicken with new green.
The ears begin to form as the grain slowly shapes.
Then, with the days and the weeks,
the whole land moves in rolling waves of gold.
The Amen of waiting becomes
the Alleluia of gathering in:
May those who sow in tears reap with shouts of joy.

Those who go out weeping,
    bearing seed for the sowing,
shall come home with shouts of joy,
    carrying their sheaves (Psalm 126:5-6).

The patience of waiting breaks into the energy
    of the harvest:
the work is hard but hearts are light—
earth has kept her promise and been faithful to us.

You crown the year with your bounty.
Abundance flows in your steps,
in the pastures of the wilderness it flows.
The hills are girded with joy,
the meadows covered with flocks,
the valleys are decked with wheat.
They shout for joy, yes, they sing (Psalm 65:9-10).

Now the grain is gathered and poured out,
to be ground and made ready for human use:
the fine white flour, the magic of the yeast,
the heat of the ovens,
the delicious fragrance of the baking...
Finally, the loaf, offered and broken as a blessing shared.

And so, day by day, we celebrate
the faithfulness of the earth and in its fruitful seasons,
the sturdy fellowship of our working together,
the quiet feast of life's steady strength.

Bread—
fruit of the earth and work of human hands—
may such a gift, become, through the blessing of God,
the Bread of true life.
May it be for us the Bread of God,
the Bread of Heaven,
the flesh of his body
given for the life of the world.
May it nourish us now
with the energies of life unending,
the harvest of the final fruits of the world.
By sharing this bread
may we be taken into him
who gave his life that we might live:
Take this, all of you, and eat it:
This is my body, which will be given up for you.

Nourished by this bread,
may we become a life-giving gift to others.
May we grow in strength to give ourselves,
laying down our lives
as grain falling into the ground,
to die, to live, not to remain alone,
but to be eaten up in humble, loving service.
Through our sharing of this bread
may the table of life be spread large and bountiful,
that all who hunger may be fed,
that all life may be welcomed and celebrated
in the joy and hope of such a meal.

The ends of the earth stand in awe at the sight
    of your wonders.
The lands of sunrise and sunset are filled with joy
    (Psalm 64:6).

We share this bread, and we raise this cup.
Blessed are you, Lord God of all creation,
through your goodness we have this wine to offer,
fruit of the vine and work of human hands.
May it become our spiritual drink.

In that earth of many blessings
the vine was planted,
its roots reaching down into that richness
from which all flowers and fruit,
all spices and fragrances,
all strength and health are drawn.
The vine grew, and we tended it,
encouraging its struggle for life and fruitfulness.
Then, the time of ripeness:
the fruit clusters in great, full, liquid bunches....
The grapes are picked,
then carted off for the pressing.
As the juices are squeezed from the fruit,
the mothering vine is left to sleep through the drear winter.
But life goes on, bubbling with secret energies,
as we wait through the time of fermentation;
then the cask of further waiting...
Finally, we draw off the fine red wine,
finding that the Spring-time promise of new life
has once more been kept.

Now is the time to toast the goodness of the earth,
our companionship in this world,
and the sharing of all the skills and arts
that makes life possible.
and to insist that life must have room for celebration...
We share the cup of our humanity
maturing over the unnumbered centuries
*   of the long struggle*
through all the living and dying,
through the tears and hopes,
the futility and fidelity,
that have gone into making this world .

Wisdom has built herself a house,....
She has mixed her wine,
she has also set her table.
She has sent out her [maids]....
"Come, eat of my bread
and drink of the wine I have mixed" (Proverbs 9:1-5).

We drink to all
who have drawn sustenance from this soil,
with whom we have shared the body of this earth—
all who have drunk their share of tears
as they suffered and sorrowed
to make this world more hopeful.
God of all care, God of all growth and fruitfulness,
Giver of all good gifts,
like the light of the sun, your face shines on the earth;
by your blessing we hold this cup:
May it become our spiritual drink!
This we offer you,
the wine of all our efforts and tears and laughter,
of all life's sufferings and lifting energies.
We offer it to you,
the life-giving God for whom we long,
that you may quench our thirst for lasting life:

Let us drink from this cup
made of the tears he wept and the blood he shed.
He drank to the full
the chalice of our human agonies,
the cup of bitter suffering
which for so many
had been life's only taste.
He drank it deeply and drank it all,
even as he prayed that it might pass—
for he thirsted for this time of rejoicing.
Blood of Christ,
pulsing with the passion of true life,
life's blood poured out in love,
shed that our joy may be complete:
this is the best wine kept till last,
now offered to those who thirst for justice on the earth,
for the forgiveness of sins,
for the refreshment and healing of all
whose hearts have been broken,
whose lives have been crushed

under the weight of the world's evils.
Let them drink from the well-springs of abundant life.

This is the cup that joins us to the true vine,
ever producing good fruit and fine wine
for the final joy of all the world.

Listen! I am standing at the door knocking;
if you hear my voice and open the door,
I will come in to you and eat with you,
and you with me (Revelation 3:20).

When we eat this bread and drink this cup,
we proclaim your death, Lord Jesus,
until you come in glory.[1]

NOTES

Chapter 1

1. *Adv. Haereses* 4, 18, 5: PG 7 /1, 1028.
2. *The Documents of Vatican II*, The Constitution on the Sacred Liturgy, #10.
3. For a fuller and most stimulating treatment of these points, see James Alison, *Raising Abel: The Recovery of the Eschatological Imagination* (New York: Crossroad, 1996).
4. A useful resource here is Hans Küng, *Does God Exist?* (New York: Random House, 1981).
5. Walter Kaufmann, ed., *The Portable Nietzsche* (New York: The Viking Press, 1968), 585–586.
6. "The New Story: Comments on the Origin, Identification and Transmission of Values," *Cross Currents,* Summer/Fall, 1987, 198–200.
7. Here I am following the suggestion, if not the wording, of Eugene La Verdiere, *The Eucharist in the New Testament and in the Early Church* (Collegeville Minn.: The Liturgical Press, 1996), 1–11.
8. Theseus's speech in *Midsummer Night's Dream*, Act 5, sc. 1.

Chapter 2

1. Saint Augustine, Sermon 272.

Chapter 4

1. For the significance of the different Greek words for eating, see F. J. Moloney, *The Gospel of John*, 224.

Chapter 6

1. For a useful overview, see Raymund Schwager, *Jesus in the Drama of Salvation: Toward a Biblical Doctrine of Redemption*, trans. James G. Williams and Paul Haddon (New York: Crossroad, 1999), 218–231.

2. Eucharistic Prayer III.

3. Eucharistic Prayer III.

4. Eucharistic Prayer III.

5. Eucharistic Prayer IV.

6. Tomas Tranströmer, "The Half-Finished Heaven," *Collected Works*, trans. Robin Fulton (Newcastle on Tyne: Bloodaxe Books, 1987), 65.

7. Teilhard de Chardin, *The Divine Milieu* (New York: Harper and Row, 1960), 123–126.

8. See Johann Baptist Metz, *The Emergent Church: The Future of Christianity in a Postbourgeois World*, trans. P. Mann (New York: Crossroad, 1981), 34–47; and G. Wainwright, *Eucharist and Eschatology* (London: Epworth Press, 1971), 80–91; 150–152.

9. For a deeply challenging treatment of the Eucharist as the sacrament of Christian community, see Francis Moloney, *A Body Broken for a Broken People* (Peabody, Mass.: Henrickson, 1997; Melbourne: Collins Dove, 1990). This book calls for a deeper discernment of ways to include in the celebration of the Eucharist those who, in the present determinations of church law, e.g., through irregularities in their marital status, are at present barred from admission.

10. Eucharistic Prayer II.

11. Eucharistic Prayer IV

12. Preface, Weekdays IV.

13. Eucharistic Prayer I.

14. Eucharistic Prayer II.

15. I refer here to the outstanding book by David F. Ford, *Self and Salvation: Being Transformed* (Port Chester, N.Y.: Cambridge University Press, 1999), especially 107–137.

16. Eucharistic Prayer I.

17. For excellent reflections on the Eucharist and the search for Christian unity, see G. Wainwright, *Eucharist and Eschatology,* 135–146.

18. See Geoffrey Wainwright, *Eucharist and Eschatology,* 78–80.

Chapter 7

1. On the nature of the sacraments as signs, see *Summa Theol.* 3, 60, 1.

2. *Summa Theol.*, 3, 75,1.

3. Eucharistic Prayer III.

4. See especially, F. X. Durrwell, *L'Eucharistie sacrament pascal* (Paris: Cerf, 1981), 89–113.

5. Hans Urs von Balthasar, *The Glory of the Lord. A Theological Aes-*

thetics. I: Seeing the Form, Erasmo Leiva-Merikakis, trans. (New York: Crossroad, 1982), 679–680.

6. See also G. Martelet, *The Risen Christ and the Eucharistic World,* R. Hague, trans. (New York: Seabury, 1976), 160–197.

7. Thomas Aquinas, *Postilla super Psalmos,* 33,8 (my translation).

Chapter 8

1. For a more thorough treatment of the ecological significance of Christian faith, see Tony Kelly, *An Expanding Theology: Faith in a World of Connections* (Sydney: E. J. Dwyer, 1993).

2. Preface, Eucharistic Prayer IV.

3. Eucharistic Prayer IV, opening words.

4. Eucharistic Prayer IV, conclusion.

5. For a sophisticated discussion of the modern situation and the value of the Eucharist, see Simon Oliver, "The Eucharist Before Nature and Culture," *Modern Theology* 15/3, July 1999, 331–353.

6. Mircea Eliade, *The Sacred and the Profane: The Nature of Religion,* Willard R. Trask, trans. (New York: Harcourt, Brace and World, 1959), 179.

7. For a wide-ranging and, I think, seminal work, see Gustave Martelet, *The Risen Christ and the Eucharist World,* trans. René Hague (New York: Crossroad, 1976).

8. A happy phrase borrowed from David S. Toolan's own splendidly "spirited" reflection, "Nature Is an Heraclitean Fire: Reflections on Cosmology in and Ecological Age," *Studies in the Spirituality of the Jesuits* 23/5, November 1991, 36.

9. Hans Urs von Balthasar, *The Glory of the Lord,* 679.

10. For a profound meditation on the relevance of classic Christian doctrines to ecological awareness, see Beatrice Bruteau, "Eucharistic Ecology and Ecological Spirituality," *Cross Currents,* Winter 1990, 499–514.

11. See *Vida y Obras de San Juan de la Cruz,* Ed., Crisogono de Jesus (Madrid: Biblioteca de Autores Cristianos, 1955), 492.

12. Peter Steele, S.J., "Praying in a Certain Place," unpublished, quoted with permission.

13. David S. Toolan, "Nature Is an Heraclitean Fire," 43.

14. B. Bruteau, "Eucharistic Ecology and Ecological Spirituality," *Cross Currents,* Winter 1990, p. 500.

15. Albert Einstein, quoted in Michael Nagler, *America Without Violence* (Covelo, Calif.: Island Press, 1982), 1.

16. B. Bruteau, "Eucharistic Ecology and Ecological Spirituality," *Cross Currents*, Winter 1990, p. 502.
17. Wendell Berry, *The Gift of Good Land* (North Point Press: San Francisco, 1981), 281.
18. David Spangler, *Emergence: The Rebirth of the Sacred* (New York: Dell Publishing Co., 1986), 81.

Chapter 9

1. Eucharistic Prayer III.
2. Eucharistic Prayer III.
3. Eucharistic Prayer III.
4. Catherine of Siena, Dialogue 78, in *Catherine of Siena. Selected Spiritual Writings*, Mary O'Driscoll, ed. (New York: New City Press, 1993), 110–111.
5. Eucharistic Prayer III.

Chapter 10

1. *Apologia*, 67:3–5, 7.
2. *Didascalia*, ch. 13.

Epilogue

1. Eucharistic Prayer I.